Indian Cooking For All

This exciting cookbook offers scores of dishes full of the exotic flavor of Indian cooking. They're easy and they're fun—and whether you're a beginner or an experienced hand, these sumptuous recipes will add new wonders of delight to you and your guests . . . and new plaudits for you!

OFF WE GO . . .
HANG ON TO YOUR MAGIC CARPET!

A Taste of India

Mary S. Atwood

 AVON PUBLISHERS OF BARD, CAMELOT, DISCUS AND EQUINOX BOOKS

The stanza from Rabindranath Tagore's poem,
"A Flight of Swans," translated by Aurobindo Bose,
was published by John Murray, London. Reprinted
by permission of the publisher.

Cover photograph decorative accessories by
Trimourti India, Inc., New York.

AVON BOOKS
A division of
The Hearst Corporation
959 Eighth Avenue
New York, New York 10019

First Avon Printing, January, 1972

AVON TRADEMARK REG. U.S. PAT. OFF. AND
FOREIGN COUNTRIES, REGISTERED TRADEMARK—
MARCA REGISTRADA, HECHO EN CHICAGO, U.S.A.

Printed in the U.S.A.

FOR MY HUSBAND

JACK

WHO WAS MY OFFICIAL FOOD-TASTER,

CRITIC AND SOUNDING BOARD

AND WHO ASSISTED ME

THROUGH EVERY PHASE OF THIS BOOK

WITH ENTHUSIASM, ENCOURAGEMENT

AND INSPIRATION

On the shores of *Bhārat*,*
Where men of all races have come together,
Awake, O my Mind!
Standing here with outstretched arms,
I send my salutations to the God of Humanity,
And in solemn chant sing His praises.
At whose call no one knows,
Came floating streams of men
And merged into the sea of *Bharat*.
The Aryan, the Non-Aryan, the Dravidian,
The Huns, the Pathans and the Moghuls —
They all have merged here into one body.
Today the West has opened its doors,
And from thence come gifts.
Giving and taking,
All will be welcome on the shores of *Bhārat*,
Where men of all races have come together.
. . . .
Come, O Aryan and Non-Aryan,
Hindu and Moslem,
Come, O English and you Christian,
Come, O Brahmin,
Purify your mind and clasp the hands of all;
Come, O downtrodden,
And let vanish all burdens of your humiliation.
Tarry not, but come you all
To anoint the Mother,
On the shores of *Bhārat*,
Where men of all races have come together.

RABINDRANATH TAGORE (1861–1941) from
A Flight of Swans, translated by Aurobindo Bose

* India

ACKNOWLEDGMENTS

THE WRITER wishes to express her thanks in particular to Mr. and Mrs. Osman Ali Khan for their most generous hospitality and inspiration, and to the following people who helped in one way or another while this book was being compiled: Mrs. Yashoda Reddy; Mr. and Mrs. Balakrishna Shetty and family; Mr. Vidya C. Shukla; Mrs. Balbir Singh; Mr. and Mrs. Adi Devitre; Mr. and Mrs. K. E. Eapen; Miss Panna Jivanlal Kilachand and her family; Mr. Tambi Kadmbavanam; Mr. and Mrs. Inder Malhotra; Mr. P. N. Seth; Mr. and Mrs. Raoof Sait; Mr. and Mrs. Mahmoud Ali; the Government of India Tourist Offices in San Francisco, New Delhi and Bombay;

and

BABOO.

CONTENTS

I   INTRODUCTION   1

II   SPICES MOST FREQUENTLY USED   11

III   OTHER BASIC INGREDIENTS   25

IV   HOW INDIAN FOOD IS SERVED
AND EATEN   32

V   RICE   37

VI   MEAT AND POULTRY   57

VII   FISH AND SEAFOOD   102

VIII   VEGETABLES   121

IX   SOUPS AND LENTILS   152

X   EGGS   164

XI   BREADS   173

XII   PICKLES, CHUTNEYS AND RELISHES   183

XIII   SNACKS   202

XIV   DESSERTS AND SWEETS   213

XV   EPILOGUE   231

GLOSSARY   235

BOOKS CONSULTED   243

INDEX   245

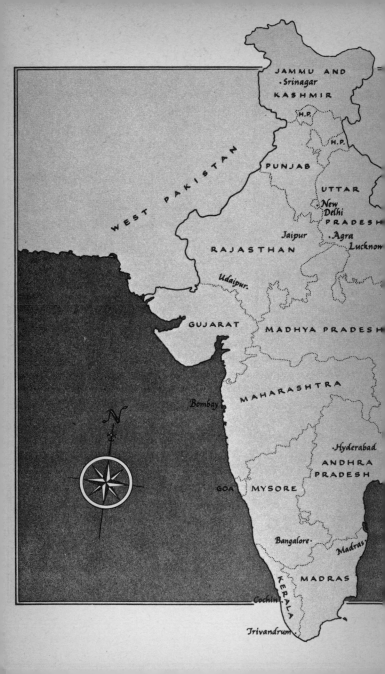

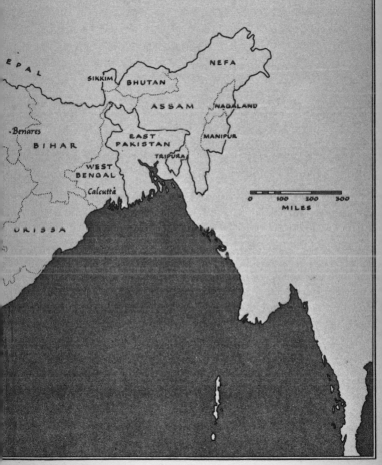

India

I. INTRODUCTION

GREAT HAVE BEEN India's gifts to the world including spices
and the art of cookery, along with the game of chess, the
decimal system, rice, cotton, sugar cane and domestic fowl.
For centuries her people have perfected their skill with spices
to transform often tasteless materials to ambrosia. Indian
cookery is not the cookery of a single nationality, however; it
dates back countless centuries and is a combination of the

cooking of many nationalities and cultures — the Greeks, Phoenicians, Chinese, Muslims, Portuguese and other Europeans. It has been influenced considerably by climatic conditions, customs, tastes, health and religions — namely Hinduism and Muhammadanism.

During the greater part of the year it is very hot in India. In many areas the temperature soars to well over 110° in the shade. With limited refrigeration facilities, meat, fish and other perishable food products would be impossible to use if they were not preserved in some way. Through the ages, it was discovered that if foods were cooked in certain combinations of spices, they would not spoil for some time. This is how spices came into use in India and why, ultimately, curries and other well-spiced foods evolved as a national cuisine. Every spice used in the various food preparations has either a preservative or an antiseptic quality. Some pungency in Indian food is considered very healthy, since perspiration is vital for cooling the body much of the year.

The use of spices, however, does not mean their use in vast amounts, nor does it mean that all Indian food is extremely hot and spicy, as many uninitiated Westerners believe. The dishes can be as hot or as mild as the individual family chooses, since this is a matter of personal taste. If an individual wishes a more piquant flavor, then Indian pickles, which are always present, can be taken. If the particular preparation seems too hot, yogurt can be added to "put out the fire."

Most people in the West refer to "curry" as if there were only one dish, instead of hundreds of them, all differing in flavor. Some are pungent while others are extremely bland, depending again on personal taste. The true art of Indian cooking lies in the subtle use and variation of spices which make each dish an exciting new experience. Indian food, however, is not just "curry." There are countless other marvelous preparations such as biryanis, pulaos, kababs and the tandoori meats and fish, to name just a few.

Another point contradicting popular belief is that a yellow cream sauce with bits of apple and yesterday's roast or leftover seafood in it (served so many times as "curry") is *not* even remotely related to Indian food. Curry and curry powder will be discussed in more detail in chapter II.

INDIAN KITCHENS AND EQUIPMENT

The kitchens in the majority of Indian homes are quite different in appearance from those of the West. There is not a great emphasis on the decorative aspects, nor on the number of appliances and gadgets. One of the reasons for this seems to be a deeply rooted instinct to avoid accumulation of material goods. This seems to be true even of the wealthier Indians who would have the means for such items. At first glance, one might feel that the Indian kitchen is a bit primitive according to our standards. However, as one begins to observe the daily food preparation, the kitchen with its equipment appears well suited to the tasks it must perform.

The most impressive sight, at first glance, in an Indian kitchen is the stack of gleaming brass *degchis* or saucepans and the row of brass canisters used for storing various staple ingredients. The degchis vary from about twelve inches to six inches in both depth and diameter, each one fitting into the other for easy storage. Both the degchis and the storage canisters can be made of aluminum or copper as well as brass, although brass is seen most frequently.

A grinding stone is another integral part of every Indian kitchen. It is about 16 or 18 inches long and 12 inches wide, with a round stone roller, like our rolling pin. It is used daily for grinding spices and pastes and frequently for lentil preparations. One exception to this is the Punjab, where a mortar and pestle is used for grinding the spices. In South India the grinding stone can also be circular.

For holding water there are earthenware jars called *jallahs* which keep the water surprisingly cool.

The Indian cook uses a very simple instrument for grating coconut, made of a circular piece of heavy metal edged with tceth and attached to a rectangular piece of wood, pointed at one end.

The other kitchen equipment includes a smooth board about two feet square for rolling out bread and a wooden roller. Then for baking the bread and for other snacks such as dosais, or for roasting coffee, which is also done at home, there is a *tawa* which is a heavy griddle about 9 inches to 12 inches in diameter. A special deep round pan called a *karahi*, with handles on either side and a heavy bottom, is the traditional pan used for deep-fat frying. Knives for chopping or cutting meat are known as *koitha* and other kitchen knives are called *choori*. Many times coconut shells with wooden handles attached are used as kitchen spoons.

Now that we are acquainted with the most common kitchen utensils, we come to the stove.

COOKING STOVES. The most universal cooking stove is the *enghatie* which is a portable little fire in a bucketlike affair, fueled with coal, coke, dung cakes, or occasionally wood. They can be used anywhere at any time, from the kitchen to the roadside. When the enghatie is used for making dishes which we ordinarily bake in a covered casserole, a method known as *dum* is employed. Live charcoal is placed on the flat lid of the pan in which the food is cooking, so that heat is then penetrating the vessel from both top and bottom and the preparation is cooking in its own steam, since the charcoal on the lid does not allow the steam to condense.

Other cooking appliances include kerosene oil stoves which are popular with the middle-class Indian, since initial expenditure is not too great and these stoves can be easily lighted and regulated. Gas, which is not available in rural areas, is used by many well-to-do Indians in cosmopolitan areas. Electricity is not popular at all, however, since the electrical current for domestic use is not reliable and the price of electrical cooking appliances and stoves is prohibitive.

THE ROLE OF WOMEN

From childhood the daughters of the family are trained for their future life — that of cooking and household management. It is interesting to observe a mother or grandmother teaching a child at play how to knead a little piece of dough or to see them encouraging her to roll it out in the form of a flat bread. For, the sooner the girl learns the better, since much of her life will be devoted to the daily tasks connected with food preparation and home management.

Without many of our Western appliances and devices the numerous household duties are very time-consuming, so the

Indian girl must readily learn how to manage efficiently *before* her marriage. She must be prepared for the seemingly endless number of her tasks, such as the purchasing of food which means going from stall to stall in the bazaar — one for vegetables, one for lentils, one for spices, another for meat, and so on. When she returns home she must clean everything, including the rice she purchases, grind the spices, and frequently grind grains into flour, unless she lives in a more urban area where this is done at a local mill. Then she must prepare all vegetables, meats, etc., for cooking, boil all the drinking water and milk, plus do the actual cooking. Cleaning and polishing the cooking utensils and vessels is another duty, as is the cleaning and care of the family's clothing. If she lives in a village she will have to carry the household water supply from the village well and will somehow have to manage to acquire the cooking fuel. Along with these duties will be the care of the children. So, with a major portion of her life to be devoted in such a way, early training is vital.

As the girl matures, her lessons increase, particularly with regard to food preparation. Each type of dish is taught over and over, until her knowledge and technique are perfect, so that as a cook, the Indian homemaker, quite naturally, is second to none and views restaurant food with great disdain. It can be easily understood how the best food in India is that found in the Indian home.

In preparing the family's food, the Indian woman finds a fulfillment for which she has been groomed from her earliest childhood, not to mention the admiration of others. For, in her cooking she brings into play all of her creative instincts which result in a work of art on the table — using her pot as the canvas and her spices and foodstuffs as the medium. Thus we see that the Indian homemaker is truly the goddess of the hearth.

CUSTOMS AND BELIEFS RELATING TO FOOD

In the Hindu home, rich or poor, there are certain rules relating to food and cleanliness which are strictly followed. Before entering the kitchen to prepare the first meal of the day, the cook must wash from head to toe and put on clean clothing. This is meticulously recorded in the Shastras, a series of books compiled centuries ago, and still carefully followed to the present day.

There is also a certain ritual related to the bath that every Hindu takes before eating his first meal of the day; not to mention the care with which hands and mouth are washed before and after eating.

The strict Indian vegetarians, who number in the millions, do not touch meat of any sort, including fish or anything that has contained a germ of life, such as eggs.

Muslims do not eat pork, although some will also not eat beef.

Vegetables, which are a principal food for many, are subject to certain taboos. Many people will not eat any vegetable whose root or stem is in the shape of a head such as mushrooms, onions and garlic. Others will not eat many of the root vegetables, which in the harvesting process might disrupt or kill any living organism in the soil.

As a rule, a respectable Hindu will not touch liquor or any

intoxicating beverage. Drunkenness is looked upon in India as very degrading. In some of the more cosmopolitan areas, however, one does occasionally see an Indian having a cocktail.

REGIONAL FOOD VARIATIONS

It is very difficult to say what is a typical Indian meal, since there are so many different eating habits and religious influences on the diet. Climatic variations play an important part, as does the economic and cultural background of the individual family in any given area.

The veneration of the cow prohibits Hindus from eating beef, but not necessarily other types of meat, such as lamb, pork, goat, chicken and other poultry — if they partake of *any* meat at all. Millions of Hindus are vegetarians, and in this group there are many contradictions: for example, those who will eat fish but not eggs, those who will eat eggs and chicken but not fish, and those who will not eat vegetables grown underground. However, strict vegetarians will not touch *anything* that has contained a germ of life.

In the North, wheat plays a large role in the diet in the form of breads such as *chappatis, parathas* and *nan*. We see the influence of the neighboring Middle East in the numbers of grilled meats such as kababs and tandoori preparations (barbecue) and the pulaos (rice dishes) which originated in Persia. Rice usually accompanies curries which can be made of either meat or vegetables. Popular in the North are *Rogan Josh*, which is a rich lamb curry, and vegetable curries such as *Aloo Matar*, which is made of potatoes and peas. *Dhals* (lentils) are very popular in this area and are eaten at almost every meal. *Raita*, seasoned yogurt, is a frequent accompaniment, along with pickles and chutneys. Desserts, usually made of milk, such as *Phirni* or one of the many halvas are very popular.

South India is noted for its vegetarian preparations and rice as the staple food. The dishes are usually hotter than in the North, and generally more coconut oil and coconut milk are used in their preparation. *Sambhar*, a hot lentil soup, served with rice, is very popular as is *Rasam*, another spicy soup with lentils as its base. In the South rice is served throughout the meal and toward the end is mixed with yogurt (for the cooling effect). *Pachadi*, seasoned yogurt, is frequently served. This is similar to the North Indian *Raita*. Popular vegetarian preparations include *Avial*, a mixed vegetable curry, *Olan*, made of squash or pumpkin and beans, and *Erisheri*, made of pumpkin and yogurt. Fish and seafoods are plentiful and are usually prepared with coconut milk. Breakfast in South India is a delightful meal usually consisting of *Idlis*, steamed rice cakes, and *Dosais*, a kind of pancake, frequently served with chutney or *sambhar*. Desserts are usually the same as those served in the North; although one especially popular one is *Payasam*, a sweet pudding-type preparation made with milk and any cereal, lentil or nut. South Indian coffee, always served with sugar and milk, is among the best in the world. It is freshly roasted and ground daily in the home and is served at any hour of the day with the greatest of pride.

In Western India we see the influence of the Gujaratis and Maharashtrians on the vegetarian foods and the Parsis and Goanese on the meat preparations. One of the unusual features of a meal in Gujarat or Maharashtra is that a sweet is served at the beginning of the meal and is eaten with a chappati or poori and various vegetables and lentils prepared as curries. The meal usually ends with rice. In general, however, less rice is eaten in the western areas than in the South or the East. Parsis and Goanese are the large meat consumers in this area. One Parsi specialty in Bombay is *Dhan Sak*, a dish made of meat and an endless list of lentils and vegetables. *Bombloe* fish, or — as we know it — Bombay duck is popular and is served either fried or curried. Various other kinds of fish such as pomfret and salmon (usually spiced and fried, although they can also be curried) are frequently served. Goanese are noted for their Vindaloo curries which are hot and sour; the spices, including plenty of red chilies, are ground with vinegar. Popular desserts include *Doodh Pak*, a milk sweet made of rice and nuts, and *Shrikhand*, a sweetened yogurt seasoned with cardamom and saffron. A well-known snack in Bombay is *Bhel Poori* which is sold by the street vendors throughout the city.

In Eastern India, Bengali fish preparations are especially popular. Both fish and rice, either plain or pulao, play an important role in the diet of the average Bengali. Fish *Kalia*, made with potatoes, peas and yogurt is very popular as is *Dahi Machi*, fish with yogurt. Mustard oil is usually the cooking medium for fish. Kathi kababs are a popular meat preparation in this area, especially with the Muslims. *Luchis*, the Bengali equivalent of the *poori*, is a frequent accompaniment to the various fish and vegetable curries served. *Rasgullas*, balls made of Indian cream cheese and flavored with rose water, are a well-known and popular sweet here.

II. SPICES
MOST FREQUENTLY USED

A number of people think that curry powder is a particular spice that is ground up, bottled and sold by the local grocer to add to a sauce, as previously mentioned; and that this sauce is then a "curry." Actually, a curry powder is a combination of spices and herbs, blended together in varying proportions. The spices found most frequently in prepared curry powders are coriander, cumin, fenugreek, turmeric, ginger, black pepper, cloves, cardamom, mace and cayenne pepper.

Commercial curry powder is *not* used in India; instead, separate spices are used, either whole or ground to a paste, to impart an individual flavor to each particular dish. Usually Indian homemakers grind their spices daily on a rectangular grindstone with another stone in the shape of a rolling pin. Then each dish will have its own unique combination of spices, thus avoiding the monotony produced by using the same mixture over and over again. Once you have tried this process of combining your own spices, you will rarely, if ever, return to commercial curry powder.

There are some other problems associated with the use of commercial curry powders. First of all, the powder is often not made from the best quality spices or the best combinations of them; and, second, even when it is, it contains a certain amount of filler, usually rice flour, which is apt to burn when it is fried and to taste burned. Thus, it is advisable to make your own *masala* or combination of spices which is easily done by whirling them together in an electric blender. Ground spices tend to lose their flavor more rapidly than those that are whole; however to grind or not to is an individual preference. You might use a mortar and pestle for this purpose, as do many Punjabis. If you do take the time to grind your spices — even cloves, cinnamon, and cardamom — you will find that they have a fresher taste than those that are ready ground.

The following are the most frequently used spices in Indian food preparation:

❧ Aniseed

Anise, an annual herb, is a native of Egypt and the Mediterranean region, and is now found in many parts of the world. The aniseed tasting of licorice is the fruit of this plant which grows to between one and two feet in height.

This herb has been used since very early times both in medicine as a carminative and in cookery. We know the ancient Greeks used it, for Pythagoras, who was born about 580 B.C. looked upon bread made with aniseed as a great delicacy.

Today it is used in breads, cakes, confectionery and in certain liqueurs, as well as in soy sauce, and is simply taken plain in small quantities after a meal in India. In Hindi it is known as *saunf*.

❧ Asafetida

Asafetida is not a direct member of the onion family but there are many similarities. It is an oleo-gum resin obtained from the fleshy roots of *Ferula foetida*, a plant found in Afghanistan and Eastern Persia. Asafetida, known as *hing* in India, is used in minute amounts in a powder form as a flavoring agent in many curries and lentil preparations.

Among its popular names are "food of the gods" and "devil's dung" due to its extreme pungency.

❧ Capsicums (Cayenne Pepper and Chilies)

Chilies, red peppers, pimientos are all fruits of varieties of the capsicum plant, a shrubby plant native to tropical America but now scattered throughout the world. There is a wide variation in size and shape of these fruits, and they range from mild to acrid in pungency.

When the Spaniards arrived in the New World, they did not find pepper such as had been found in the Orient, but they did find these indigenous and rather pungent fruits which they called *pimienta* (the Spanish name for pepper), and to distinguish them from the pepper from India they added the Mexican name *chili* to make "chili pepper." Later the peppers were called capsicums by botanists because the hot seeds were enclosed in a capsule.

The Portuguese carried the seeds to India, and from there they were spread throughout the Orient.

The pungency of cayenne pepper depends on two things: the variety of capsicum dried and used, and the removal or otherwise of the seeds. Usually the small, red-hot bird peppers are used for cayenne. In general, the smaller the pepper, the more pungent it will be. The larger red peppers are used in making chili powder and paprika.

Since chilies and red peppers are all fruits of the many varieties of the capsicum plant, it is well to clarify some of the differences in the products on your grocer's shelf. Cayenne pepper is the hottest spice since it is made of the small, red-hot bird peppers; it usually consists of the whole pod and seeds ground together to form this fiery powder. Chili powder may be very hot or can be relatively bland, depending entirely on the particular pepper which is used. In purchasing chili powder for use in Indian preparations it is important to carefully check the label to be sure that the product is *pure* chili powder. *Under no circumstances* use chili powder that has other ingredients in it, such as oregano, garlic, allspice, cloves, etc. This blended chili powder is meant to be used in chili con carne and various Mexican dishes, and its use in Indian food preparations would be disappointing to say the least. Pure chili powder can be purchased in many large supermarkets as well as in most oriental and Mexican food shops. It is usually labeled as to the degree of hotness. Let your taste and that of your family be your guide in such a case; however, ideally, the medium hotness would be best to use in the preparations in this book to maintain maximum authenticity.

✍ Cardamoms

Cardamoms, a member of the ginger family, are the ripe fruit of a large herbaceous plant native to India and Ceylon. It is the little seeds inside the fruit capsules which form this highly aromatic spice, which was known to Indian and Arabic writers in very early times. Susruta, the Indian writer mentions it under the Sanskrit name "Eta" about the eighth century. Today we find most of the Indian names of the spice are derived from this form, such as *elachi* in both Hindi and Bengali.

Cardamoms are also mentioned in the list of spices liable to duty at Alexandria during the years A.D. 176 to 180. Along with most other spices of the day, it had a reputation as an aphrodisiac.

The seeds are much used in India as a flavoring, particularly in pulaos and biryanis as well as in the majority of sweets.

It is better for the seeds to be kept in their capsules until ready for use, so they will retain their aromatic eucalyptus-scented properties. Thus great importance is attached commercially to the appearance of the capsules which are bleached and sometimes coated lightly with starch.

The major supply of cardamom comes from the areas of Mangalore and Mysore in India and from Ceylon.

❧ Cinnamon

The cinnamon tree, a member of the laurel family, is a native of Ceylon and the Malabar coast of India. It seems to have been one of the earliest known spices and is often mentioned in the Old and New Testaments.

In the wild state this tree grows up to 40 feet high, but cultivated it does not exceed about 8 feet. The trees are cut off to form stools from which emerge shoots that are then allowed to reach a certain size before they, in turn, are cut off and the bark is slit lengthwise. The pieces of bark are packed together, one within another, to form solid sticks about ½ inch wide and a yard long, then these are graded. The sticks are known as "cinnamon quills" commercially; "quillings" are the broken pieces and "featherings," the small leftover pieces of bark. The trees are ready for commercial production in about five years, and after about eighteen years the bark is of little use.

Cinnamon is used either whole or powdered. In Hindi it is known as *darchini*.

❧ Cloves

The earliest record of the clove is in Chinese books dating from 266 to 220 B.C., when officers of the court were required to hold cloves in their mouths when addressing their sovereign. From the eighth century onward this spice was regularly exported to Europe, but was extremely costly.

Cloves are the unopened flower buds of the clove tree, a

member of the myrtle family, indigenous to a small number of islands in the Moluccas, but later introduced into Zanzibar and Pemba, Madagascar, Penang, Ceylon and other tropical areas.

The clove tree, with shining green leaves and rosy flowers, is usually about 12 to 20 feet tall, but in some places it attains a height of 40 feet. Its aromatic leaves bear tiny oil glands, the scent of which can be detected from a considerable distance on hot, still nights. Rumphius (1626–1693) wrote in his *Herbarium Amboinense* that the clove tree was "the most beautiful, the most elegant and the most precious of all known trees."

The young trees begin to bear about the fifth year and may go on bearing for fifty years or more. The flower buds appear in January or February and are ready for picking about July. The buds are first white, then green and finally bright red. When the base of the bud begins to turn red, the picking begins. As the buds are not all ripe at once, it is necessary to go over the trees two or three times during the harvest season.

The buds, after picking, are spread out on mats or cement drying floors for four to five days. Another method used, since they must be rapidly dried, is to plunge them into boiling water and then expose them to smoke and heat until they take on a brownish color. The sun-dried cloves are of better quality.

The resemblance of the dried buds to nails has given them their name in many languages. The English word "clove" is derived from the French *clou* (a nail) and the same idea occurs in the Spanish *clavo* and the Italian *chiodo*. In Sanskrit the name is *laoango,* and in Hindi *laung.*

◆§ *Coriander*

Coriander, the aromatic seed of a herbaceous annual, is indigenous to the Mediterranean region and the Caucasus and is extensively cultivated in Northern India. It is one of the oldest known spices, being mentioned in the Ebers papyrus and in Sanskrit literature, as well as in the Bible as resembling manna (Exodus and Numbers). Its use as an aphrodisiac is referred to in the *Thousand and One Nights*.

As a spice, coriander forms an important ingredient of curries and curry powders, and the green leaves are used extensively as a garnish and in some chutneys. In the West this aromatic seed is used for flavoring confectionery and gin.

The name "coriander" is derived from the Greek word *coris*, meaning a bug, since the ancients compared the smell of the green plant, both leaves and seed, with that of bugs. When dried the seed has a most agreeable odor. In Hindi it is known as *dhannia*.

◆§ *Cumin*

Cumin is the aromatic, dried ripe fruit of a herbaceous annual plant, a native of the Mediterranean region, North Africa, and Arabia, and now widely cultivated. It is quite a small plant, rarely exceeding 12 inches in height. The fruit is about ¼ inch long and is grayish-brown, containing a white seed.

Cumin was well known to the ancients, and is mentioned by Isaiah as well as in the works of Hippocrates, Dioscorides and Theophrastus. During the Middle Ages it was a popular spice for fowl.

It is used extensively in India in curries and savories and is very popular in all Oriental cooking. In Hindi it is known as *jeera*.

≈§ Fenugreek

Fenugreek seed is really a pulse, but is used as a spice because of its aroma. Native to the Mediterranean area, this annual is now extensively cultivated in North Africa, India and Pakistan. In common with other members of the pea family, it develops pods in which are found little, flat, almost square seeds marked with a deep furrow. These are the seeds of commerce, and small they are, it taking some 2,500 of them to make an ounce.

Fenugreek is used in chutneys and curries and is one of the ingredients of curry powder. In Hindi, it is known as *methi*.

≈§ Ginger

Ginger is the pungent underground stem of a herbaceous perennial plant which was one of the earliest oriental spices known to Europeans. Marco Polo saw its cultivation in India and China between 1271 and 1292. Its original home is unknown, as no one seems ever to have met with it in a wild state anywhere.

It is propagated from cuttings of the rhizome or underground stem, each containing a bud, from which a new plant develops. After flowering, they are dug up, washed, scraped and dried in the sun. When the skin is left on, it is called "coated"; when it is removed, "uncoated" or "scraped."

The name "ginger," coming from *Zingiber*, seems to be derived from the Sanskrit *Sanjabil*. In Hindi it is known as *adrak* when green and as *sont* when dry.

In India the fresh ginger plays an important part in curry as well as many other food preparations. It is one of the most popular flavoring agents known and has been so used for many centuries in both the East and the West.

Fresh ginger root (green ginger) has an important place in Indian cooking. It can be found in many Chinese, Japanese and Puerto Rican markets. An inch of the root will yield about one tablespoon of minced ginger. Where fresh ginger is not available, powdered ginger may be substituted, but keep in mind that the taste will not be the same as with the fresh. One inch of fresh ginger equals about ¼ teaspoon of the dry powdered kind. Another substitute for fresh ginger is bottled stem ginger. To use this, wash the desired amount and chop finely.

◄§ Mace. See Nutmeg and Mace

◄§ Mustard

Mustard is one of the oldest known medical and culinary herbs, frequently being mentioned in the Bible. There are two mustards of commercial importance — black and white. Both have bright yellow flowers which make a mustard field in bloom a lovely and unforgettable sight.

The black and white mustards are rather similar in appearance, but the pods of the black are only about ½ inch long and contain much smaller seeds than those of the white whose pods are about 2 inches long. To compare the approximate sizes of the seeds: it takes about 5,000 whole white seeds to make up an ounce, and over 12,500 of the black seeds are needed for the same weight. The seeds of the black mustard produce a more pungent, volatile oil.

Vast quantities of mustard are grown in India where mustard seed oil is used for cooking, particularly in Bengal. Mustard seeds are used for flavoring in a variety of Indian dishes. In Hindi, mustard is known as *rai*.

◆§ Nutmeg and Mace

The nutmeg tree is native to the eastern islands of the Moluccas known as the Spice Islands and is cultivated in Malaya, throughout Indonesia, in western New Guinea and in parts of the West Indies.

The first record of nutmegs in Europe is in a poem written about 1195 by Petrus D'Ebulo, describing how at the entry of the Emperor Henry VI into Rome, before his coronation, the streets were fumigated with nutmegs and other aromatics.

The nutmeg tree is a somewhat bushy tree, about 30 to 50 feet in height. The fruit when ripe is one of the most beautiful in nature. About 2 to 2½ inches in length, the fruit is oval, smooth and pale orange-yellow with a groove running down one side. When quite ripe, the fruit splits almost in half along the groove. Within the parted husk is the seed which is the nutmeg of commerce. Over this seed lies a crimson network, the arillus, an outgrowth from the base of the seed, closely wrapping it to the top. This is the mace of commerce, when dried. Good trees average between 1,500 to 2,000 nuts a year; they do not reach their highest bearing capacity, however, until about twenty years of age.

In India, nutmeg is used in puddings and in some curries. Mace is used in sweet dishes such as *halvas* as well as in betel nut mixtures used after eating and between meals. Nutmeg is known as *jaiphul* in Hindi, and mace is known as *javitri*.

ᴇᴇᴦ Pepper

Both black and white peppers are products of the same plant, a perennial vine, native to the forests of Travancore and Malabar in India and now extensively cultivated in Malaya, Indonesia, Thailand, Viet Nam, the Philippines, and the West Indies.

Black and white peppers are the dried fruits of *Piper nigrum,* the pepper of commerce. White pepper is merely the smooth ripe seed of the black pepper freed from the outer coat of skin by soaking in running water for about a week which accelerates the loosening process. Black pepper is stronger and more aromatic than white since part of the pungency is in the skin. Since the removal of the husks results in a considerable loss of weight, white pepper is naturally more expensive.

The so-called red pepper or cayenne is not a true pepper. It is made from a capsicum. Among other spices to which the name pepper is applied are Jamaica pepper, which is allspice or pimento, and Melegueta pepper or Guinea pepper.

Pepper is a product of nature which has exercised a profound effect upon the world of commerce. During the Middle Ages pepper was the most valued spice, and Venice, Genoa, and other European cities owe much of their wealth to the importation of this spice. Taxes and tributes were often paid in pepper. Thus in the siege of Rome by Alaric, king of the Goths, the ransom of the city was 5,000 pounds of gold, 30,000 pounds of silver, and 3,000 pounds of pepper; and after the conquest of Caesarea by the Genoese in A.D. 1101 each soldier was rewarded with 2 pounds of pepper.

The pepper berries are borne in clusters on hanging stems

or spikes and receive different treatment according to whether black or white pepper is wanted. For black pepper the spikes are gathered when they are just turning red before they are completely ripe and are spread on mats to dry in the sun. Care is taken to dry them rapidly to prevent mold or mildew. In the preparation of white pepper the spikes are allowed to ripen more than for black pepper, that is, until nearly all of the berries are showing red color.

There are many varieties of pepper, the best of which is, perhaps, Balamcotta, from Tellichery in South India. Lampong is a generic name denoting the white pepper from that area. Saigon pepper refers to that coming from Viet Nam.

In Hindi, black pepper is known as *Kali Mirch*.

~§ Saffron

The saffron of commerce consists of the dried stigmas and tops of the styles of the flowers of a member of the iris family. Saffron's original home is unknown, but it is believed that it probably came from Asia Minor where it has grown for centuries, although it has long been cultivated in Spain from where most of our saffron comes today.

It was mentioned in the Song of Solomon as the *karcom* of the Hebrews and eventually found its way to the Western world through the returning Crusaders. For centuries it has been a culinary herb, highly regarded for its therapeutic virtues as well. It also served in olden times as a dye, but this use is no longer general, due to its cost and tendency to fade. In India, however, it still colors bridal veils and ceremonial garments.

In harvesting, the flowers are collected and the orange-red

stigmas and upper parts of the styles are separated and dried. Its costliness can, perhaps, seem more understandable if it is known that it takes between 300,000 and 400,000 stigmas to make one pound of dried saffron. In Indian cookery, golden saffron's warm and slightly bitter aroma is used to flavor and color a number of pulaos and biryanis. It is known as *kesar* in Hindi.

◆§ Turmeric

Turmeric is an underground root belonging to the ginger family. Although it has long been cultivated in India and has a Sanskrit name, no one seems to have met with it growing in a wild state.

In the Middle Ages turmeric was known as Indian saffron, and when first introduced into Europe it was used almost exclusively as a dye. Even today in many parts of India, one will be told simply that this yellow spice is "saffron" which can result in confusion unless one actually sees for oneself the particular spice spoken of and identifies it. (See also *Saffron*, page 23.)

The roots, thick and rounded, are of a gray or yellowish exterior color and deep orange or red on the inside. After harvesting, the roots are washed, heated in earthenware pots, and then dried in the sun for a week or two.

India is one of the largest consumers of turmeric and vast quantities go into curries to give many of them their typical brilliant yellow color. Most of it comes from Madras and Bengal states. The name of turmeric in Hindi is *haldi*, taken from the Sanskrit name, *haridra*.

III. OTHER BASIC INGREDIENTS

ALTHOUGH they play a large part in Indian cookery, we must remember that spices are not its only distinguishing ingredients. There are coconut milk, yogurt, tamarind (or our substitute, lemon juice) and clarified butter — to name just a few others which add to the special nature of Indian food.

It is a fallacy to imagine that the ingredients necessary for Indian food are not readily obtainable in the United States;

they are nearly all to be had at your leading grocer's, super-market, gourmet shop or health food store. Some items could be ordered by mail from the leading gourmet shop. If you are at a complete loss, you might inquire at the Government of India Tourist Offices in the larger cities where certain items are obtainable.

☙ Coconut and Coconut Milk

Coconut milk is essential in many Indian preparations. To prepare it, use only *unsweetened* or fresh coconut, *not* the packaged sweetened variety. You will find many health food stores that carry unsweetened coconut. But, if at all possible, use fresh coconut.

The best way to open a fresh coconut: Heat your oven to 350°. Punch a hole in the "eyes" of the coconut and drain off the liquid which you can later use as a part of the liquid requirement for coconut milk. Place the coconut in the heated oven for 15 minutes. Remove. If the shell has not already cracked, knock it with a hammer.

Please note: The liquid inside the fresh coconut is *not* coconut milk.

To prepare the grated coconut: Cut off the inner brown skin and dice the meat. Put in an electric blender and whirl to desired texture.

For thick coconut milk: Combine 1 cup of grated unsweet-ened coconut with 1 cup of milk, plus the liquid from the fresh coconut if you are using one. The coconut liquid is optional. Bring the coconut and milk just to a boil in a heavy saucepan. Remove from heat and let stand ½ hour. Strain before using.

For thin coconut milk: Combine 1 cup grated unsweetened coconut, 1 cup milk, 1 cup water and coconut liquid if you are using a fresh one. Bring just to a boil in a heavy saucepan. Remove from heat and let stand ½ hour. Strain before using.

If for any reason, you are forced in an emergency to use the sweetened variety of coconut — WASH the required amount well in cold water to remove the sweetness before proceeding.

◄§ Green Chili Peppers

Green chili peppers add considerable "heat" to Indian food preparations. Their size varies from about 1 inch to 4 or 5 inches. In the recipes where one green chili is called for, use one of about 1½ inches to 2 inches, and omit the seeds, if you wish, to cut down on the hotness; or add the whole green chili to the dish while it is cooking and then remove and discard it after the food has been flavored. If you wish, you might substitute green pepper to derive the flavor without the hotness. Or if green chilies, fresh or canned, are not available, you could substitute green pepper and cayenne pepper or crushed red pepper to your taste. Mexican and Italian markets usually have these items year round.

◄§ Fresh Coriander Leaves

Fresh coriander leaves, also known as Chinese parsley or *cilantro*, are widely used throughout India in many food preparations, and also frequently serve as a garnish as we use regular parsley. Many Westerners dislike their distinctive smell and taste. If this is the case, you can omit them entirely or substitute a mixture of equal parts of chopped regular parsley and chives. You can find fresh coriander leaves in many Chinese and Mexican markets, or you can easily grow the plant in your herb garden.

✑ Fats and Oils

Many different fats and oils are used for cooking in India, depending on the budget and the region. Coconut oil and sesame seed oil are popular in the South; while in Bengal a lot of mustard seed oil is used, particularly when cooking fish. Throughout India much of the finest food preparation is done with *ghee* or clarified butter. Once you discover the many advantages of this product, you will use it regularly in all of your cooking. First, it does not burn at higher temperatures as ordinary butter does. This is because the milky particles which ordinarily blacken when regular butter is heated are removed. Another point is that with the absence of this milky residue, the butter will keep much longer without becoming rancid.

To make clarified butter: Place about 2 pounds of butter in a heavy saucepan over moderate heat. When the butter is melted, skim off the foam and remove from the heat. Strain the remaining yellow liquid through a tea towel, discarding the milky residue in the bottom of the pan. Store in a covered jar or dish in the refrigerator. This may seem like quite an operation, but it is well worth the time and effort.

Clarified butter is the preferred fat for Indian food preparation. Margarine, however, can be substituted for butter in many of the recipes in this book by those watching their cholesterol consumption. Be sure to take care to prevent burning, if it is used.

In the majority of recipes vegetable oil, also, can be used, if it is preferred to butter. Peanut oil is excellent in most of the recipes, although almost any of the various vegetable oils could be used except olive oil which is *never* used in Indian cooking.

❧ Lentil and Rice Flours

Lentil flour can be prepared from Egyptian lentils, split peas, chick-peas or even lima beans. Place the lentils or peas in an ungreased, heavy frying pan and brown them over moderate heat, stirring constantly to prevent burning. Cool. Put them into an electric blender and pulverize them. Sift and store in a tightly covered jar.

Rice flour can be prepared the same way; however, do not brown the rice. Stir it until it just begins to change color. Then cool and proceed as above.

Rice and lentil flours can be obtained at many health food stores.

❧ Poppadums

Most gourmet food shops as well as many large supermarkets throughout the United States now carry poppadums which are usually marketed in small packages or boxes. To prepare them for use: heat vegetable oil an inch or more deep in a skillet and fry them, one at a time, until puffed and crisp. The frying time will be very short, so you must work quickly. Drain on absorbent paper.

These wafers are the most universal bread and can be served with virtually any curry or food preparation in this book except some of the Snack preparations.

Shopping List

aniseed

asafetida

cardamoms

cayenne pepper

chili pepper, green

chili powder (*pure*)

cinnamon

cloves

coconut, grated unsweetened

coriander, dry

coriander leaves, fresh

cumin

fenugreek seeds

flour (lentil and rice)

ginger, powdered

ginger root, fresh

mace

mustard seeds

nutmeg

paprika

pepper, black and white

poppadums

poppy seeds

saffron

sesame seeds

turmeric

dhal (lentils)

SUMMARY OF
EQUIVALENTS AND SUBSTITUTIONS

1-inch piece of fresh ginger	Equals 1 tablespoon of minced fresh ginger *or* about ¼ teaspoon dry powdered ginger.
Juice of 1 large lemon	Equals juice of 1 small lime in acidity.
1 cup uncooked rice	Yields about 2¾ to 3 cups cooked rice.
Green chilies	Substitute green pepper for mildness *or* green pepper and cayenne pepper to taste.
Fresh coriander leaves	Substitute equal parts of chopped parsley and chives.
Cayenne pepper *or* red chili powder	Substitute paprika for mildness without a color sacrifice.

IV. HOW INDIAN FOOD
IS SERVED AND EATEN

INDIAN FOOD is usually served to each person on a circular tray about twelve inches in diameter which is called a *thali*. This thali can be made of brass, copper, silver or stainless steel and takes the place of a table setting. A series of small metal cups called *katoris*, holding vegetables, meat, yogurt, pickles and melted butter line the edge of the thali. Rice and bread, such as chappatis, are put directly onto the tray itself, usually in the middle. A metal tumbler for water completes the setting.

The hands and mouth are washed before sitting down to eat and again after the meal.

The food is eaten with the forepart of the first two fingers and the thumb of the right hand. The left hand is used for other cleaning purposes and so is considered unclean for touching food. Thus, only water in the metal tumbler or a glass can be taken with the left hand.

Each person must take care not to touch or to drop any food particles on the thali of one's neighbor, since this is considered unhygienic and the thali would then have to be removed and replaced by a fresh one.

The vast majority of India's population do not use knives and forks. It is thought that these implements are quite unsuitable to Indian food. Many of the more orthodox Hindus cannot understand how we can use forks again and again after having once put them in our mouths. Even though they have been thoroughly washed and cleaned, knives and forks are considered unclean by many.

Some orthodox Hindus will not use plates and serving dishes at their meals, believing them to be unhygienic. So their foods are served on banana leaves or the leaves of certain trees sewed together.

Frequently, banana leaves will be used as plates, especially in the South, at large gatherings such as weddings to facilitate the serving and cleaning up operations — as we in the West occasionally use paper plates.

INDIAN MEALS

Depending on the affluence of the family, an Indian meal is ·*generally* made up of:

> rice and a curry
>
> *dhal* (cooked lentils) or a cooked vegetable
>
> *poppadums* or other bread such as *chappatis, parathas* or *pooris*
>
> pickles, such as mango or lemon
>
> yogurt
>
> a sweet

The courses are not separated in India. The dishes are placed on the table or on a large tray in an orderly manner and the individual can choose freely what he desires. Melted butter and salt are two items that are always available to be sprinkled or poured over whatever dish one might desire.

The villagers' diet is considerably different from the meal just listed. By necessity it is generally limited to the simplest foods: rice, dhal (lentils), chappatis, yogurt or milk, tea or coffee with sugar.

Many people have the mistaken idea that chopped peanuts, sieved hard-cooked egg and grated coconut are necessary toppings for a curry. These are not authentic Indian accompaniments! In this same vein, Major Grey's chutney, although manufactured in India (for export), is not used in Indian homes. Indian chutneys are more frequently those made up daily which are listed in the Pickles, Chutneys and Relishes chapter of this book.

There also seems to be considerable confusion as to the best beverages to serve with an Indian curry. To be authentic you would serve only water. Alcoholic beverages are taboo, not only with a meal but at any time, in India. For those who would prefer another form of refreshment, you might serve beer or a Pimms cup. Do not serve wine. It is not correct, nor does it enhance the flavors of Indian food. The meal could be followed by either tea or coffee. The use of tea is more prevalent, although coffee is popular in South India where it is grown.

Frequently, after the hands and mouth are washed at the conclusion of a meal, betel nut wrapped with spices in a *paan* leaf is passed. These wrapped morsels are popped into the mouth and munched with gusto for some time by both men and women as the finale to the meal. In the United States you might pass tiny cups of grated coconut, aniseeds, and cardamom as a similar refreshment and finale.

The following are some menus that will give an idea of the many, many possibilities of combinations in an Indian meal.

SUGGESTED MENUS

Rogan Josh	Samosas
Rice	Tandoori Chicken with
Dhal	Onion Slices and Lime
Fried Green Beans	Wedges
Onion Raita	Palak Sag
Lemon Pickle	Nan
Carrot Halva or Phirni	Kulfi

Murgh Masalum
Plain Pulao
Seasoned Okra
Chappatis or Parathas
Mango Pickle
Yogurt
Gulab Jamon

Malayalee Fish Pappas
Rice
Ginger Curry
Kerala Theeyal
Poppadums
Yogurt
Jallebis or Banana Halva

Vegetarian

Sambhar
Rice
Spicy Eggplant
Spinach with Yogurt*
Tomato Pachadi
Poppadums
Cashew Nut Halva

* Omit the egg if necessary

V. RICE

RICE, one of the oldest and most extensively cultivated grain cereals in the world, is the staple diet for the majority of India's population, particularly in the South. As you travel northward, however, you see wheat incorporated into the diet of the North Indian in the form of *chappatis* and related breads, although rice still maintains a substantial importance.

We are told that in India alone there are more than a thou-

sand varieties of rice. Some of the more well-known are *patna,
pulao, chamar, rangoon, ruphsal, dadghani* and *basmati*. We
might compare the knowledge and care with which an Indian
selects his rice to that of an epicurean selecting his wine. He
immediately recognizes the variety by its shape, texture, color
and — with a quick sniff of a handful — by its "bouquet" or
fragrance. In general, patna rice is the kind used regularly by
the well-to-do Indians.

In India, the states where rice is grown in vast quantities
are Madras, Kerala, Orissa, Bengal and Bihar. In the rice-
growing areas, particularly, it is common to see a small bundle
of rice hung on the entrance to an Indian home or a temple.
This comes from the first harvest of the season and signifies
prosperity.

During a Hindu wedding, raw rice in a brass dish, topped
with yellow-dyed coconut, is present along with the sacred fire
and several oil lamps. On one occasion during the ceremo-
nies, the bridegroom ties a handful of rice in the bride's sari;
and on another occasion toward the end of the marriage rites,
the couple shower each other with handfuls of red-colored
rice. The rice used during these rituals symbolizes the wish
that the couple may enjoy an abundance of this world's goods
and that their union will be fruitful.

Indian rice dishes defy comparison, ranking among the most
delectable rice preparations in the world. Quite apart from
regular steamed rice are the heavenly and exotic Indian pulaos
and biryanis — seemingly an endless number of combinations
of rice, butter, spices, meat, fish, and vegetables.

Pulao, a specialty of the Mogul kings, originated in Persia
and is known in some form throughout the world as *pilaff,
pilau* or the distinctive Indian *pulao*. For pulao, the rice is

first fried in clarified butter and then steamed. The addition of spices and other items depends on the individual choice, tastes of the family, or the pocketbook.

Biryanis are the "royalty" of rice preparations and the dish to serve on the most auspicious occasions. They are often the main course during formal entertaining and are always served to welcome houseguests on the first day of their visit. Biryanis are made by arranging half-cooked rice in layers with meat, poultry, fish, or vegetables in a heavy casserole. Butter and saffron are sprinkled over the top, the lid is sealed on, and the dish is baked to blend all of the flavors and finish cooking the rice. Before serving, the preparation is garnished with sautéed nuts, raisins, fried onion rings, quartered eggs, or sometimes very thin gold or silver foil and rose water. Truly a feast for a king!

Everyone seems to have a favorite method for preparing steamed rice. Many people soak it in cold water before cooking, while others feel that rice should not even be washed. It is entirely a matter of individual choice; however, unless the rice you are using is covered with talc, the rice marketed in the United States is clean enough so that washing and soaking is not really necessary in the majority of cases.

It is always preferable to use old rice, since new rice has a tendency to become sticky or soggy. If there is some question of this, you can add 1 tablespoon of butter to the boiling water for every 1½ cups rice used. Another point, ALWAYS use long-grain rice!

You will have success with your rice every time if you follow these rules:

1. For each cup of rice, use double the amount of water.
2. Always use boiling water.

3. Add butter to the boiling water, if there is some question as to the age of the rice.

4. Stir the rice only upon its addition to the boiling water; fluffing it at the end of the cooking period.

5. Keep the lid of the pot on and don't continually peek at it.

6. Keep the heat constant and low after adding the rice; however, it must continue to boil or you will have mushy rice.

The amount of raw rice to cook always seems to create a question. Remember that 1 cup of rice yields about 2¾ to 3 cups of cooked rice. You can then judge the amount according to your individual requirements and the appetites of your family and guests. In India the size of the rice serving usually varies in inverse proportion to the amount of other foods available with the meal.

Plain Boiled Rice

2 cups long-grain rice   4 cups water
1½ teaspoons salt

Bring water to a full boil. Add salt and rice. Stir to break up any lumps of rice. Cover tightly, lower heat, and simmer until rice is cooked and water has evaporated. Depending on your rice, this will be between 14 and 20 minutes.

Lime Rice

¼ cup clarified butter
½ teaspoon mustard seeds
1 bay leaf, crumbled
1 teaspoon turmeric
1 cup chopped cashew nuts
½ teaspoon cayenne pepper
1 teaspoon salt

2 cups rice, half-cooked and drained
1 cup grated unsweetened coconut
1 tablespoon chopped coriander leaves, optional
juice of 4 limes

Heat butter and fry mustard seeds until they pop. Add bay leaf, turmeric, chopped cashew nuts, cayenne pepper, and salt. Fry over very low heat for 3 minutes, stirring constantly. Add to rice, along with coconut, coriander leaves, and lime juice. Cover tightly and put in a 350° oven for 15 minutes.

Egg Rice

3 cups boiling water
1½ teaspoons salt
4 cloves
¼ teaspoon crushed black pepper
4 eggs, beaten

pinch ground cinnamon
1½ cups long-grain rice
4 tablespoons melted clarified butter
1 small onion, finely chopped

Add salt, cloves, black pepper, and cinnamon to boiling water. Then add rice and stir well. Cover and steam until rice is done.

Meanwhile, in a large skillet, sauté onion in butter until brown. Add beaten eggs, cook for 30 seconds to 1 minute. Add hot rice. Stir well and remove from heat. Serve very hot.

Yogurt Rice

1½ cups yogurt	¼ teaspoon cayenne pepper
1 cup buttermilk	4 cups cooked rice, at room
1 teaspoon salt	temperature
1 tablespoon minced green	2 teaspoons vegetable oil
pepper	1 teaspoon mustard seeds
½ teaspoon grated ginger	1 bay leaf, crumbled

Combine yogurt, buttermilk, salt, green pepper, grated ginger, and cayenne pepper. Mix thoroughly. Combine with rice.

Heat vegetable oil and fry mustard seeds and crumbled bay leaf until seeds pop. Stir into rice. Serve cold with pickles.

In India, this dish is prepared the last thing at night and eaten at noon the next day. It is especially refreshing during hot weather.

Tomato Rice
(Tomato Bhath)

4 tablespoons clarified butter	⅛ teaspoon crushed black
2 medium onions, thinly sliced	pepper
3 cloves garlic, crushed	1½ cups long-grain rice
1 teaspoon finely chopped	1½ teaspoons salt
ginger	3 cups tomato juice
4 cloves	

3 tablespoons fresh coriander leaves

Fry onions until brown in the butter. Remove half of the onion for use as a garnish. Add garlic, ginger, cloves, and

black pepper to remaining onion in skillet. Fry ....
Add rice and fry for 2 or 3 minutes.

Combine tomato juice and salt. Bring to a boil. Add rice, stir well and cover tightly. Steam until done over low heat. Serve garnished with browned onion and chopped fresh coriander leaves. *Note:* You may substitute chives and parsley for the coriander leaves.

Yellow Rice

¼ cup clarified butter
2 medium onions, thinly sliced
1 teaspoon turmeric
pinch of cumin
3 cloves
coriander leaves, optional
⅓ cup grated unsweetened coconut
1½ teaspoon salt
2 cups long-grain rice
4 cups boiling water

Sauté onions in the butter until golden. Add turmeric, cumin, cloves, and coconut. Fry for a minute or two. Add rice and stir for two minutes. Add to boiling, salted water. Stir well and cover. Steam until rice is done. Serve garnished with coriander leaves, if desired.

Rice and Eggplant
(Vangi Bhath)

5 tablespoons vegetable oil
2 teaspoons ground coriander
1 teaspoon cumin
1 teaspoon chili powder
1 teaspoon crushed mustard
    seeds
¼ teaspoon turmeric
pinch asafetida, optional

¼ teaspoon crushed black
    pepper
1 pound eggplant, peeled and
    sliced
1½ teaspoons salt
2 tablespoons lime juice
¼ cup water
3 cups hot, cooked rice

Heat oil and fry the coriander, cumin, chili powder, mustard seeds, turmeric, asafetida, and black pepper for 2 or 3 minutes. Put in eggplant slices and fry for 5 minutes. Sprinkle with salt and lime juice. Add water and simmer until water has evaporated and eggplant is tender. Combine with hot rice. Mix well and serve.

Sesame Rice

4 tablespoons clarified butter
2 tablespoons cashew nuts
1 cup sesame seeds
½ teaspoon cayenne pepper
1 bay leaf, crumbled

1 teaspoon salt
4 cups hot, cooked rice
juice of ½ lime or
    1 tablespoon rose water

Sauté cashews until golden brown in 1 tablespoon of the butter. Remove and set aside. Add remaining 3 tablespoons of butter and fry the sesame seeds, cayenne, and bay leaf until the seeds are a golden brown.

Combine the cashew nuts and fried sesame seeds. Stir into the hot, cooked rice along with the salt. Mix thoroughly. Sprinkle on the lime juice and serve.

Coconut Rice

1½ cups grated unsweetened coconut
4 cups water
¼ cup clarified butter
1 small onion, thinly sliced
2 tablespoons chopped green pepper
1 clove garlic, crushed
2 whole cardamoms
4 cloves
1-inch stick of cinnamon
2 teaspoons salt
½ cup cashew nuts, coarsely chopped
¼ teaspoon cayenne pepper
2 cups long grain rice
1 large tomato, peeled and chopped

Combine 1 cup of the coconut with the 4 cups water and bring to a boil. Remove from heat and let stand for 20 minutes. Strain, reserving the liquid for cooking the rice. Be sure to press out all excess moisture from coconut.

Melt butter and sauté onion until golden. Add chopped green pepper, garlic, cardamoms, cloves, cinnamon, salt, cashew nuts, and cayenne pepper. Fry for 2 or 3 minutes. Add rice and stir for another 3 minutes.

Meanwhile bring the reserved coconut liquid to a boil and add the tomato, remaining ½ cup of coconut, and the hot, sautéed rice mixture. Stir. Cover tightly and steam until the rice is done.

Potatoes, Cauliflower and Rice

¼ cup clarified butter	1 cup long-grain rice
6 cloves	1 teaspoon turmeric
1-inch stick of cinnamon	¼ teaspoon aniseed, powdered
1 bay leaf, crumbled	1½ teaspoons salt
3 small potatoes, peeled and quartered	2 cups water
	crushed black pepper to taste
1 small head cauliflower, cut into flowerets	chili powder to taste

Heat butter and fry the cloves, cinnamon, and bay leaf for a minute or two. Add potatoes, cauliflower and rice. Fry for 2 minutes. Add turmeric and aniseed. Stir well and fry 2 minutes.

Bring water to a boil, add salt and fried rice mixture. Stir well. Cover tightly, lower heat and steam until done.

Just before serving, add crushed black pepper and chili powder. Toss gently and serve very hot.

Plain Pulao

¼ cup clarified butter	2 cups long-grain rice
¼ teaspoon turmeric	3¾ cups boiling water or hot stock
4 whole cardamoms	
4 cloves	2 teaspoons salt
1 bay leaf, crumbled	2 tablespoons raisins
2-inch stick of cinnamon	2 tablespoons almonds
2 teaspoons clarified butter	

Heat ¼ cup butter and fry the turmeric, cardamoms, cloves, bay leaf and cinnamon for a minute or two. Add rice and fry for 2 or 3 minutes, stirring constantly. Stir rice into boiling, salted water. Cover and steam until rice is cooked.

Meanwhile, fry raisins and almonds in butter for 1 or 2 minutes.

Serve rice garnished with sautéed raisins and almonds.

This pulao can be garnished with small *koftas* (meatballs), see Kofta Curry, page 59.

Tomato Pulao

⅓ cup grated unsweetened coconut
1¼ cups water
3 whole cardamoms
3 cloves
1 bay leaf, crumbled
1 small onion, grated
2 teaspoons finely chopped green pepper
¼ cup chopped fresh coriander leaves
½ teaspoon turmeric
1½ cups long-grain rice
3 tablespoons clarified butter
1 tablespoon clarified butter
2 cups tomato juice
2 teaspoons salt
1 tablespoon raisins
1 tablespoons cashew nuts

Combine grated coconut and water. Bring to a boil, remove from heat, and let stand ½ hour. Strain and squeeze out as much liquid as possible, reserving liquid.

Meanwhile, heat butter and fry cardamoms, cloves, and bay leaf for a minute or two. Add onion, green pepper, coriander leaves, turmeric, and rice. Fry for 2 or 3 minutes.

Combine extracted coconut liquid, tomato juice, and salt. Bring to a boil and stir in the rice mixture. Cover, lower heat. Steam until done.

While rice is steaming, sauté cashew nuts and raisins in 1 tablespoon clarified butter.

Serve pulao hot, garnished with the nuts and raisins.

You may substitute chopped parsley and chives for the coriander leaves.

Shrimp Pulao

4 tablespoons clarified butter
1 large onion, thinly sliced
1 tablespoon ground coriander
1 teaspoon cumin
¼ teaspoon turmeric
1 teaspoon chili powder
pinch of ground cloves
pinch of ground cinnamon
pinch of ground cardamom
1 teaspoon salt

2 large tomatoes, peeled and chopped
2 cups shrimp, peeled and deveined
¼ cup yogurt
1 teaspoon minced parsley
3 cups hot, cooked rice
2 tablespoons melted clarified butter

Fry onion in 4 tablespoons butter until golden brown. Add coriander, cumin, turmeric, chili powder, cloves, cinnamon, and cardamom. Fry for 2 or 3 minutes. Add tomatoes and salt. Cook for 5 minutes. Put in shrimp and fry for 5 minutes. Stir in yogurt and parsley.

Butter a casserole. Alternate layers of rice and shrimp, ending with a layer of rice. Sprinkle on melted butter. Cover tightly. Seal edges of casserole with aluminum foil and place in a 350° oven for 20 minutes.

Green Pea Pulao

5 tablespoons clarified butter	1 bay leaf, crumbled
1 medium onion, thinly sliced	1½ cups long-grain rice
6 cloves	1 cup green peas
3 whole cardamoms	2 teaspoons salt
3-inch stick of cinnamon	3 cups water

Heat 2 tablespoons of the clarified butter and fry the onion
until brown. Remove and set aside for garnishing. Heat remaining 3 tablespoons of the butter and fry the cloves, cardamoms, cinnamon, and bay leaf for a minute or two. Add rice,
fry for 2 or 3 minutes, add peas and fry for one more minute.

Heat water to boiling point. Add salt and rice-pea mixture.
Stir well. Cover and steam until done.

Serve garnished with browned onion.

Pulao with Lamb

1 pound lean lamb, cubed	2-inch stick of cinnamon
2 medium onions, quartered	4 whole cardamoms
2-inch stick of cinnamon	1 bay leaf, crumbled
3 cloves garlic	1 teaspoon turmeric
½-inch piece of ginger, sliced	½ teaspoon cumin
1 tablespoon minced green pepper	½ teaspoon cayenne pepper
⅛ teaspoon cayenne pepper	1 cup long-grain rice
1 teaspoon salt	1 teaspoon salt
4 cups water	½ cup yogurt
¼ cup clarified butter	2 cups lamb stock
2 medium onions, thinly sliced	2 hard-cooked eggs, sliced
6 cloves	1 tablespoon rose water, optional

Combine lamb cubes, quartered onions, 2-inch stick cinnamon, garlic, ginger, green pepper, ⅛ teaspoon cayenne, 1 teaspoon salt, and water, and simmer about 1 hour. You can tie the spices in a cheesecloth bag, if you prefer, for easier removal. Strain. Remove lamb cubes and set aside. Skim fat off stock. This portion of the recipe can be done a day ahead and chilled for easier fat removal. Discard cooked spices and vegetables.

Sauté sliced onions in clarified butter until brown. Remove and set aside for use as a garnish. Add cloves, remaining stick of cinnamon, cardamoms, and bay leaf. Fry for 1 minute. Add turmeric, cumin, and ½ teaspoon cayenne, and fry one more minute. Put in lamb cubes and brown them, adding more butter, if necessary. When meat is brown, add the salt and rice. Fry for 2 minutes. Mix in the yogurt and fry another 2 minutes.

Bring 2 cups of the lamb stock to a boil and add fried lamb and rice. Stir well. Cover tightly, lower heat and steam until rice is done.

Serve garnished with browned onion and sliced hard-cooked eggs. Sprinkle with rose water, if desired.

Vegetable Pulao

8 tablespoons clarified butter	2 whole cardamoms
2 medium onions, thinly sliced	1-inch stick of cinnamon
2 tomatoes, peeled and quartered	2 cloves
	1 bay leaf, crumbled
½ cup green peas	¼ teaspoon crushed black pepper
½ cup green beans, sliced	
½ cup cauliflower, cut up	1½ cups long-grain rice
½ cup carrots, thinly sliced	3 cups water
2 teaspoons salt	

Heat 2 tablespoons of the butter and brown the onions. Remove and set aside for garnishing.

Add 3 tablespoons butter to pan. Put in tomatoes, peas, green beans, cauliflower, and carrots. Fry for 5 minutes. Remove and set aside. In remaining 3 tablespoons of butter, fry the cardamoms, cinnamon, cloves, bay leaf, and pepper for 2 minutes. Add rice and fry for 2 or 3 minutes.

Bring the water to a boil and add salt. Put in vegetables and rice. Stir well. Cover tightly, lower heat, and let steam until rice is done. Serve garnished with browned onions.

Chicken Biryani

1 frying chicken, disjointed, 2 to 2½ pounds	¼ teaspoon ground cloves
1½ cups yogurt	¼ teaspoon ground cinnamon
juice of 1 lime	¼ teaspoon ground cardamom
4 cloves garlic, crushed	3 large onions, sliced
2 teaspoons grated ginger	¼ cup clarified butter
1 tablespoon ground coriander	1½ teaspoons salt
1 teaspoon cumin	3 cups half-cooked rice
¼ teaspoon cayenne pepper	¼ teaspoon saffron
¼ teaspoon crushed black pepper	2 tablespoons warm milk
	¼ cup sautéed cashew nuts
	2 hard-cooked eggs, quartered

Combine the yogurt with the lime juice, garlic, grated ginger, coriander, cumin, cayenne pepper, black pepper, ground cloves, cinnamon, and cardamom. Mix thoroughly and combine with chicken parts. Set aside to marinate for 2 hours.

Brown onions in butter and combine with the chicken in a large, heavy casserole. Add salt and simmer over very low heat about 1 hour or until chicken is tender.

Remove half of the chicken. Spread half of the rice over the chicken in the casserole; add the other half of the chicken, and then the remaining rice. Sprinkle with the saffron which has been dissolved in the milk. Cover tightly, seal edges with aluminum foil and place in a 300° oven for 35 minutes.

Serve garnished with sautéed cashew nuts and quartered hard-cooked eggs.

Moglai Biryani

1½-inch piece of ginger
3 cloves garlic
¼ cup blanched almonds
½ teaspoon cayenne pepper
6 tablespoons clarified butter
2 medium onions, thinly sliced
1½ pounds lamb, cubed
2 teaspoons salt
1 cup water
1 bay leaf, crumbled
¼ teaspoon ground cardamom
¼ teaspoon ground cloves
¼ teaspoon ground cinnamon
¼ teaspoon turmeric
1 tablespoon chopped mint
leaves

1 fresh or pickled green chili, finely chopped, or 2 teaspoons minced green pepper
2 tablespoons chopped fresh coriander leaves, or 1 tablespoon parsley and 1 tablespoon chives
juice of 1 lime
1 cup yogurt
3 cups half-cooked rice
4 tablespoons milk
¼ teaspoon saffron
butter
rose water

Grind together the ginger, garlic, almonds, and cayenne pepper in a food mill or electric blender.

Heat 3 tablespoons of the butter and brown the onions. Remove onions and set aside. Heat remaining 3 tablespoons of butter and fry the ground ginger-nut paste for 2 or 3 minutes. Add the lamb, sprinkle with 1 teaspoon salt, and fry until brown. Put in water, cover and simmer about 1 hour.

Meanwhile in a bowl, combine the bay leaf, cardamom, cloves, cinnamon, turmeric, remaining teaspoon salt, mint leaves, green chili, coriander leaves, lime juice, and yogurt. Mix well. When lamb cubes are tender and very little gravy remains, add spiced yogurt. Stir well.

Butter a heavy casserole. Put in layers of lamb, browned onion, and rice. Repeat until all ingredients are used. Dissolve the saffron in 1 tablespoon of the milk. Pour the remaining 3 tablespoons milk over the top of the casserole. Then sprinkle on the saffron milk. Dot with butter. Cover tightly. Seal edges of the casserole with flour-and-water paste or with aluminum foil. Put in a 300° oven for 40 minutes. Sprinkle with rose water before serving.

Fish Biryani

1 pound fish fillets, halibut or cod	2 teaspoons ground coriander
¾ cup yogurt	pinch of ground cinnamon
1½ teaspoons salt	pinch of ground cloves
2 cloves garlic, crushed	pinch of ground cardamom
1 teaspoon grated ginger	3 cups hot half-cooked rice
2 teaspoons chopped mint leaves	1 large tomato, peeled and thinly sliced
	3 tablespoons melted butter

Combine yogurt, salt, garlic, grated ginger, mint leaves, coriander, cinnamon, cloves, and cardamom. Mix thoroughly and combine with fish. Set aside for 1 hour to marinate.

Grease a heavy casserole and alternate layers of rice, fish, and tomato, ending with a layer of rice. Sprinkle on melted butter. Cover tightly and seal casserole edges with aluminum foil. Place in a 300° oven for 35 to 40 minutes.

Lamb Biryani

Meat:

1½ pounds lamb, cubed	3 tablespoons grated unsweet-
1 cup yogurt	ened coconut
4 tablespoons clarified butter	2 tablespoons ground coriander
2 medium onions, finely	1 teaspoon chili powder
chopped	1 teaspoon salt
1 teaspoon grated ginger	¼ cup water
2 cloves garlic, crushed	¼ teaspoon ground cloves
2 tablespoons minced green	¼ teaspoon ground cinnamon
pepper	¼ teaspoon ground cardamom
¼ teaspoon crushed black pepper	

Rice:

3 tablespoons clarified butter	1-inch stick of cinnamon
1 small onion, sliced	1½ cups long-grain rice
2 cloves	1 teaspoon salt
2 whole cardamoms	3 cups water

Topping:

1 tablespoon rose water

Garnish:

2 hard-cooked eggs, sliced

Meat: Combine lamb cubes with ½ cup yogurt and set aside. Melt butter and fry the onions until golden. Add ginger, garlic, green pepper, coconut, coriander, chili powder, and salt. Fry for two or three minutes. Add lamb cubes and brown them, adding more butter, if necessary. Add remaining ½ cup yogurt and ¼ cup water. Simmer until lamb is very tender and not much gravy remains. When done, sprinkle with ground cloves, cinnamon, cardamom, and black pepper.

Rice: Heat butter and brown the onion. Add whole cloves, cardamoms, cinnamon stick, and fry for a minute or two. Add rice and fry another two minutes. Bring water to a boil. Add salt and fried rice. Cover and steam until done.

Biryani: Butter a casserole. Alternate layers of lamb and rice, ending with a layer of rice. Sprinkle top with rose water. Cover and place in a 200° oven for 15 minutes. Serve garnished with hard-cooked eggs.

Kitchri

¼ cup split yellow peas soaked 1 hour	2 cloves
	1 teaspoon salt
boiling water	pinch of turmeric
1 cup long-grain rice	2¼ cups water
2 whole cardamoms	2 tablespoons melted butter

Cover split peas with boiling water and cook for 15 minutes. Drain.

Bring 2¼ cups water to a boil. Add cardamoms, cloves, salt, and turmeric. Stir in rice and drained split peas. Cover tightly, lower heat, and steam until done.

Before serving, sprinkle with melted butter. Serve with poppadums.

In India there are any number of lentils that might be used in kitchri instead of the split peas. Usually, however, *toor dhal* is used in the proportion of 1 part to 3 parts rice. You can use any lentil you wish in this recipe. But, be sure you know its cooking time (by cooking it once, first). Some lentils do not need parboiling; others do.

Variation: Garnish with a cup of cooked green peas or browned onion rings.

VI. MEAT AND POULTRY

THE MULTIPURPOSE COW is a creature of special privilege in modern day India. In Hinduism, the cow is a symbol of the earth, the nourisher; this sanctity evolving, perhaps, from her centuries of life- and food-giving attributes. Although the Hindu veneration of this creature restricts the beef consumption in India, this prohibition does not give Hindus a distaste for all forms of flesh.

Lamb is the most often used meat throughout India, while goat is eaten fairly generally in the rural areas. Chicken runs a close second to lamb, and is considered a festive delicacy. Although beef has not been mentioned in most of the following recipes, it can easily be substituted in the majority of cases.

The meat and poultry cookery in India takes many forms, not only that of curry. One of the closest competitors to the curry method is that of *tandoori*-cooking, a form of barbecue.

The *tandoor* is a cylindrical clay oven which can stand from four to five feet high or, occasionally, is buried in the sand. Once the fire is burning properly, it is banked at one side for the actual cooking process. During this period the sand and ashes covering the bottom absorb much of the dripping fat without flaming or smoking. The sides of the vessel narrow toward the top to form a mouth about one foot in diameter. Spiced meat or poultry, either whole or in kabab form, and occasionally fish, are placed on greased skewers and quickly thrust within to cook in the intense heat generated. Frequently *nan*, an oblong Indian bread, is cooked on the inside walls of the tandoor at the same time.

It is fascinating to watch the cook, poised over the mouth of the oven, waiting for just the right moment to thrust in the skewered meat or with moistened hands to quickly shape the bread and slap it on the inside wall.

Indian meat curries take many forms. There is the *kofta*, made of ground meat shaped into round balls and cooked in a sauce; or fried, baked or broiled. There is the *Meat Korma*, a rich, spicy, thick curry made of plenty of yogurt and butter; and *Rogan Josh*, one of the most popular North Indian meat dishes, with a deep red, aromatic sauce. Then, there is the *Keema Curry* which is made of ground meat in a thick sauce, with green peas and hard-cooked eggs frequently added.

There are many, many curries — each one better than the previous. Don't be afraid to experiment. Let yourself go, for you and your family can enjoy a taste of the beautiful and exotic India right in your own home.

Kofta Curry

Meatballs:

1½ pounds ground lamb or beef
2 tablespoons chopped coriander leaves
1 teaspoon salt
1½ teaspoons grated ginger
⅛ teaspoon ground cloves
⅛ teaspoon ground cinnamon
1 teaspoon flour
1 egg, beaten
3 tablespoons vegetable oil

Curry:

3 tablespoons vegetable oil
1 medium onion, thinly sliced
1 tablespoon ground coriander
1 teaspoon paprika
¼ teaspoon crushed red pepper
¼ teaspoon turmeric
2 cloves garlic, crushed
juice of ½ lemon
2 teaspoons green pepper, minced
2 tablespoons grated unsweetened coconut
1 teaspoon salt
3 large tomatoes, peeled and chopped
½ cup boiling water

Combine ground lamb or beef, coriander leaves, salt, ginger, cloves, cinnamon, flour, and beaten egg. Wet hands and shape mixture into even-sized meatballs. Sauté in the vegetable oil until browned. (If coriander leaves are not available, substitute 1 tablespoon chopped parsley and 1 tablespoon chives.)

For the curry, heat the remaining 3 tablespoons of vegetable oil and fry the onion. Add ground coriander, paprika, red pepper, turmeric, garlic, green pepper, and coconut. Fry for 2 or 3 minutes. Add salt, tomatoes, and boiling water. Simmer for 12 to 15 minutes. Put in browned meatballs and simmer 10 minutes. Just before serving, sprinkle with lemon juice.

Spicy-fried Lamb I

2 small onions	3 tablespoons vegetable oil
½ teaspoon grated ginger	3 cloves garlic, crushed
¼ teaspoon cumin	⅛ teaspoon ground cloves
¼ teaspoon turmeric	1 teaspoon salt
1 teaspoon cayenne pepper, or to taste	2 tablespoons water
	juice of ½ lime
2 pounds lamb shoulder, cut in 1-inch cubes	

Grate one of the onions and combine with the grated ginger, cumin, turmeric, and cayenne. Add this spice-paste to meat, mixing well.

Thinly slice remaining onion. Sauté until golden along with the garlic in the vegetable oil. Add ground cloves and fry for a minute or two. Put in spiced meat. Sprinkle with salt. Cover and slowly fry for 30 minutes. Sprinkle on water and continue frying, uncovered, until meat is tender and water has evaporated. Five minutes before removing from heat, add lime juice.

Note: A Teflon pan is excellent for the preparation of this dish.

Spicy-fried Lamb II

3 tablespoons coconut oil
2 large onions, thinly sliced
1 tablespoon fresh or pickled green chilies, finely chopped
4 cloves garlic, crushed
1 teaspoon ginger, finely chopped
¼ cup chopped coriander leaves or 2 tablespoons each parsley and chives
2 pounds lamb shoulder, cut in 1-inch cubes
2 large tomatoes, peeled and chopped
1 teaspoon salt

Heat the oil and fry the onions until golden. Add the green chilies, garlic, ginger, and coriander leaves. Fry for 2 or 3 minutes. Put in lamb cubes and fry 5 minutes. Add tomatoes and salt. Cover and cook, stirring occasionally, until lamb is tender and most of moisture has evaporated.

Note: If coconut oil is not available, use vegetable oil or clarified butter.

Nargisi Meatball Curry
(Nargisi Kofta Curry)

Meatballs:

1 pound finely ground lamb
2 eggs
¼ teaspoon ground cinnamon
¼ teaspoon ground cardamom
¼ teaspoon ground cloves
¼ teaspoon cayenne pepper, optional
1 teaspoon salt
4 hard-cooked eggs, shelled
flour
3 tablespoons vegetable oil

Curry:

2 medium onions, thinly sliced	1 teaspoon turmeric
3 tablespoons vegetable oil	1 teaspoon salt
3 cloves garlic, crushed	½ cup tomato paste
2 fresh or pickled green chilies, finely chopped	1½ cups boiling water
	fresh coriander leaves, chopped

Combine ground lamb, raw eggs, cinnamon, cardamom, cloves, cayenne pepper, and salt. Mix well. Dip the hard-cooked eggs in flour and coat with the ground meat mixture. Heat vegetable oil and carefully fry meatballs until brown.

Meanwhile, brown onions in the other 3 tablespoons vegetable oil. Add garlic, green chilies, and turmeric. Fry for 3 minutes. Add salt, tomato paste, and boiling water. Simmer for 15 minutes.

Cut the meatballs in half and gently put into the sauce with the yoke side up. Simmer until heated through. Garnish with chopped fresh coriander leaves.

Lamb Korma Curry

2 tablespoons ground coriander	1 teaspoon paprika
1 teaspoon cumin	6 cloves
1 tablespoon poppy seeds	¼ teaspoon ground cardamom
1 teaspoon turmeric	2 medium onions
4 cloves garlic	2 pounds lamb, cubed
1-inch piece ginger	3 tablespoons vegetable oil
¼ teaspoon cayenne pepper	2-inch stick of cinnamon
1 fresh or pickled green chili	1 teaspoon salt
3 tablespoons grated unsweet- ened coconut	1 cup yogurt
	water

Grind together in a food mill or electric blender the coriander, cumin, poppy seeds, turmeric, garlic, ginger, cayenne pepper, green chili, coconut, paprika, cloves, cardamom, and one of the onions.

Heat vegetable oil and brown the remaining onion which has been thinly sliced. Put in the cinnamon stick and the ground-spice paste. Fry for 3 minutes. Add meat and fry for 5 minutes. Put in salt and yogurt. Cover and simmer slowly until meat is tender, adding just enough water to keep it from burning and to form a thick gravy.

North Indian Lamb Curry
(Rogan Josh)

3 tablespoons vegetable oil	pinch of ground cloves
1 large onion, thinly sliced	pinch of nutmeg
3 cloves garlic, crushed	pinch of mace
1 tablespoon grated ginger	pinch of saffron
2 tablespoons ground coriander	2 pounds leg of lamb, cubed
1 tablespoon poppy seeds, crushed	½ cup yogurt
	1½ teaspoons salt
1 teaspoon cumin	3 large tomatoes, peeled and chopped
1 teaspoon turmeric	
1 teaspoon paprika	½ cup water
¼ teaspoon ground cardamom	fresh coriander leaves or parsley
½ teaspoon cayenne pepper	

Heat oil and brown the onion. Add garlic, ginger, coriander, poppy seeds, cumin, tumeric, paprika, cardamom, cayenne pepper, cloves, nutmeg, mace, and saffron. Fry for 3 minutes. Put in lamb cubes and fry for 5 minutes. Stir in yogurt. Then add salt, tomatoes, and water. Cover and simmer until meat is tender and sauce is thick. Serve garnished with chopped coriander leaves or parsley.

Jammu Lamb

5 tablespoons vegetable oil	4 cloves
3 large onions, sliced	1 teaspoon cumin
2 pounds lamb, cubed	1 teaspoon paprika
½ cup yogurt	1 teaspoon vanilla
1 bay leaf	½ teaspoon saffron
2-inch stick cinnamon	1½ teaspoons salt
1 teaspoon grated fresh ginger	1 cup hot water

Brown onions in 2 tablespoons of the oil and set aside. In remaining 3 tablespoons of oil, brown the meat. Add yogurt. Simmer until yogurt is absorbed. Add fried onion, bay leaf, cinnamon, ginger, cloves, cumin, paprika, vanilla, saffron, and salt. Stir thoroughly. Add hot water, cover, and simmer about 1 hour until done, adding more water if it becomes too dry.

North Indian Lamb and Kidneys

1 pound lamb cubes	¼ teaspoon powdered cardamom
8 lamb kidneys, cleaned and sliced	1½ cups water
2 teaspoons grated fresh ginger	1 teaspoon salt
6 cloves garlic, crushed	2 onions, thinly sliced
½ teaspoon chili powder	1 cup yogurt
5 tablespoons vegetable oil	¼ teaspoon saffron
8 cloves	3 hard-cooked eggs, quartered

Combine lamb cubes, kidneys, ginger, garlic, and chili powder. Set aside to marinate for 1 hour. In 3 tablespoons of the oil, fry the cloves and cardamom for a minute or two. Add lamb and kidneys. Brown lightly. Pour in water and add salt. Cover and simmer until tender.

Meanwhile, in remaining 2 tablespoons of oil, brown the onions. Mix them with yogurt and saffron. When meat mixture is cooked, add the yogurt mixture, stirring well. Simmer for 10 minutes. Garnish with hard-cooked eggs.

Stewed Lamb with Tomatoes and Potatoes

2 pounds stewing lamb	⅛ teaspoon ground cardamom
water	⅛ teaspoon ground cinnamon
2 tablespoons vegetable oil	1 teaspoon chopped mint leaves
1 large onion, thinly sliced	1 teaspoon chopped coriander
4 cloves	leaves, optional
1 teaspoon cumin	1½ teaspoons salt
½ teaspoon aniseed, crushed	2 large tomatoes, peeled and
¼ teaspoon crushed black	chopped
pepper	2 large potatoes, peeled and
¼ teaspoon chili powder	quartered
juice of ½ lime	

Simmer lamb in enough water to cover for 1 hour. Skim off excess fat.

Heat vegetable oil and brown the onion. Add cloves, cumin, aniseed, black pepper, chili powder, cardamom, and cinnamon. Fry for two or three minutes. Add to lamb. Put in mint leaves, coriander leaves, if used, salt, and tomatoes. Simmer for 20 minutes. Add quartered potatoes and cook until done. Stir in lime juice just before serving.

Lamb with Cauliflower

3 tablespoons vegetable oil
2 medium onions, thinly sliced
4 teaspoons ground coriander
1 teaspoon chili powder
½ teaspoon turmeric
1 teaspoon finely chopped ginger

1½ pounds lamb, cubed
1½ teaspoons salt
2 large tomatoes, chopped
¼ cup yogurt
1 cup water
1 small head cauliflower, cut into flowerets

Heat vegetable oil and brown onions. Add ground coriander, chili powder, turmeric and ginger. Fry for 2 or 3 minutes. Put in lamb and fry for 5 minutes. Add salt, tomatoes, yogurt and water. Mix well. Cover and simmer for about 30 minutes. Add cauliflower and continue simmering for another 30 minutes, until very tender.

Baked Marinated Lamb

12 cloves
5 whole cardamoms
¼ teaspoon black peppercorns
1 cup yogurt
pinch of saffron
1 teaspoon grated ginger
1 teaspoon chili powder

2-pound leg of lamb, cubed
¼ cup clarified butter
2 bay leaves
1 tablespoon raisins
2 tablespoons slivered blanched almonds
1½ teaspoons salt

Whirl together the cloves, cardamoms and peppercorns in an electric blender. Combine with the yogurt, along with the saffron, ginger and chili powder. Add lamb, mixing thoroughly. Set aside for 1 hour to marinate.

Melt butter in a heavy casserole. Put in lamb and yogurt mixture. Add bay leaves, raisins, almonds and salt. Cover and seal on lid with flour-and-water paste or with strips of aluminum foil. Bake in a 350° oven for about 1½ hours.

Fried Lamb and Coconut

½ coconut	¼ teaspoon ground cinnamon
5 tablespoons clarified butter	¼ teaspoon aniseed
pinch of turmeric	¼ teaspoon ground cloves
1 small onion, thinly sliced	¼ teaspoon crushed black
½ teaspoon ginger, finely chopped	pepper
2 tablespoons ground coriander	2 bay leaves, crumbled
½ teaspoon chili powder	1½ pounds lamb, cut in ½-inch cubes
¼ teaspoon turmeric	1 teaspoon salt

Slice coconut into strips about ¼-inch wide and 1 inch long, leaving brown skin on. Heat 1 tablespoon of the clarified butter. Put in the coconut strips, sprinkle on a pinch of turmeric, and sauté for 5 minutes. Set aside.

Heat remaining clarified butter and fry onion until golden. Add ginger, coriander, chili powder, turmeric, cinnamon, aniseed, cloves, black pepper, and bay leaves. Fry for 2 minutes. Add lamb cubes, salt, and coconut strips. Cover and cook over low heat until meat is tender, stirring frequently.

Indian Style Lamb Stew

1½ pounds stewing lamb	1 tablespoon clarified butter
2 cups water	2 cloves garlic, crushed
3 medium onions, sliced	½ teaspoon ginger, finely
6 cloves	chopped
2-inch stick of cinnamon	1 teaspoon coriander leaves,
1 teaspoon salt	finely chopped
1 cup green peas	

Combine the lamb, water, onions, cloves, cinnamon, and salt. Simmer until meat is tender. Skim off excess fat.

Fry garlic, ginger, and coriander leaves in butter for 2 or 3 minutes. Add to lamb along with green peas. Simmer until peas are tender.

If desired, substitute 1 teaspoon chives for coriander leaves.

Keema Curry

3 tablespoons vegetable oil	⅛ teaspoon ground cardamom
1 large onion, finely chopped	1 bay leaf, crumbled
4 cloves	1 pound ground lamb
1 tablespoon green pepper, minced	1 teaspoon salt
1 teaspoon turmeric	2 large tomatoes, peeled and chopped
1 teaspoon chili powder or to taste	1 cup boiling water
¼ teaspoon ground cinnamon	1 cup green peas
¼ teaspoon crushed black pepper	3 hard-cooked eggs, halved
	2 tablespoons coriander leaves, chopped

Brown onion in vegetable oil. Add cloves, green pepper, turmeric, chili powder, cinnamon, black pepper, cardamom and bay leaf. Fry for 3 minutes. Put in meat and fry for 5 minutes, stirring well to break up the lumps. Add salt, tomatoes and boiling water. Simmer for 30 minutes. Add peas. When peas are almost done, add hard-cooked eggs. Serve garnished with chopped coriander leaves, or substitute chives and parsley.

Lamb-Stuffed Cucumbers

Stuffing:

2 tablespoons vegetable oil	½ teaspoon salt
1 medium onion, minced	¼ teaspoon crushed black
¼ teaspoon ginger, finely chopped	pepper
	1 teaspoon chopped mint
pinch of ground cinnamon	leaves
pinch of ground cloves	½ pound ground lamb

Cucumbers:

3 medium cucumbers	1 teaspoon paprika
3 tablespoons vegetable oil	¼ teaspoon turmeric
2 medium onions, thinly sliced	¼ teaspoon crushed red pepper
1 teaspoon cumin	1 teaspoon salt
½ cup boiling water	

Stuffing: Brown the minced onion in the vegetable oil. Fry ginger, cinnamon, cloves, salt, black pepper and mint leaves for 2 or 3 minutes. Add lamb, stirring well to break up lumps and fry for 5 minutes.

Peel cucumbers. Cut off a small piece at one end and remove seeds. Fill up hollow with fried ground lamb, leaving about a ¾-inch space at end.

Heat remaining 3 tablespoons of vegetable oil and brown the sliced onions. Add cumin, paprika, turmeric, crushed red pepper and salt. Fry for 2 or 3 minutes. Add hot water and bring to a boil. Put in stuffed cucumbers, lower heat and simmer until tender.

Muslim Style Leg of Lamb (Raan)

2 tablespoons grated ginger	1 tablespoon ground coriander
5 cloves garlic, crushed	½ teaspoon cayenne pepper
½ cup yogurt	½ teaspoon ground cloves
1½ teaspoons salt	½ teaspoon ground cinnamon
¼ teaspoon black pepper	½ teaspoon ground cardamom
juice of 1 lime	4½–5-pound leg of lamb

Combine ginger, garlic, yogurt, salt, black pepper and lime juice. Make several small gashes in the leg of lamb with a sharp knife. Spread the yogurt mixture over the entire surface. Put in a roasting pan and set aside for 1 to 2 hours, to marinate.

Combine coriander, cayenne pepper, cloves, cinnamon and cardamom in a small skillet and stir over moderate heat for 3 or 4 minutes. Set aside to cool.

When ready to roast, sprinkle the combined spices over the lamb and put into a 350° oven for about 2 hours. In India this popular Muslim dish would be cooked over an open fire with live charcoal on the lid of the pan.

Lamb Do Pyaz

4 large onions	½ teaspoon cayenne pepper
4 teaspoons ground coriander	¼ teaspoon turmeric
2-inch stick of ginger	3 tablespoons vegetable oil
3 cloves garlic	2 pounds lamb shoulder, cubed
½ teaspoon paprika	1½ teaspoons salt
½ teaspoon cumin	1 cup boiling water

Grind together 2 of the onions, coriander, ginger, garlic, paprika, cumin, cayenne pepper, and turmeric in a food mill or electric blender.

Thinly slice remaining 2 onions. Heat vegetable oil and brown onions. Add spice paste and fry 2 or 3 minutes. Put in lamb shoulder cubes and fry about 10 minutes. Sprinkle with salt. Add boiling water and simmer until tender.

Lamb Indad

3 tablespoons vegetable oil	2-inch stick of cinnamon
1½ pounds lamb or beef, cubed	¼ teaspoon ginger, finely
1 large onion, finely chopped	chopped
4 cloves	¼ teaspoon crushed red pepper
1 teaspoon paprika	3 cloves garlic, crushed
¼ teaspoon turmeric	1¼ cups water
½ teaspoon cumin	2 tablespoons vinegar
1 teaspoon salt	

Heat vegetable oil and brown lamb cubes. Remove and set aside. Put in the chopped onion and brown it. Then add cloves, paprika, turmeric, cumin, cinnamon, ginger, crushed red pepper and garlic. Fry for 2 or 3 minutes. Put in browned lamb cubes, water, vinegar and salt. Simmer until lamb is tender, about 1 hour.

Mild Lamb Curry

2 pounds lamb, cubed
6 cloves garlic, crushed
3 medium onions, thinly sliced
4 tablespoons vegetable oil
2 teaspoons ground coriander
1 teaspoon cumin
½ teaspoon paprika
½ cup yogurt
½ teaspoon ginger, finely chopped
¼ teaspoon cayenne pepper
pinch of ground cardamom
1½ cups water
1½ teaspoons salt
½ teaspoon sugar

Mix together the lamb cubes and crushed garlic. Set aside 1 hour.

Heat vegetable oil and fry onions until golden. Add coriander, cumin, paprika, ginger, cayenne pepper and ground cardamom. Fry for 2 minutes. Put in lamb and fry for 5 minutes. Add water and bring to a simmer. Add salt and sugar. Cover and simmer until meat is tender. Just before serving, stir in the yogurt.

Cooked Lamb and Potatoes
(Jhal Faraezi)

3 tablespoons vegetable oil	½ teaspoon turmeric
2 large onions, finely chopped	2 cups cold, cooked lamb, diced
½ teaspoon cayenne pepper	2 medium potatoes, cooked and
½ teaspoon crushed black pepper	diced
	1 teaspoon salt
juice of ½ lime	

Heat oil and fry onions until brown. Add cayenne pepper, black pepper, turmeric, meat, potatoes, and salt. Mix thoroughly. Fry about 5 minutes. Sprinkle on lime juice and continue cooking for another 2 or 3 minutes.

Note: Other cooked, cold meat can be substituted for lamb.

South Indian Lamb Curry

2 medium onions	2 tablespoons grated unsweetened coconut
1 fresh or pickled green chili	
½ cup fresh coriander leaves	pinch of ground cinnamon
1-inch piece ginger	pinch of ground cloves
1 teaspoon chili powder	3 tablespoons vegetable oil
2 cloves garlic	2 pounds lamb, cubed
2 teaspoons ground coriander	1 cup yogurt
1 tablespoon poppy seed	1½ teaspoons salt
1 cup water	

Grind together one of the onions, green chili, coriander leaves, ginger, chili powder, garlic, ground coriander, poppy seed, coconut, cinnamon, and cloves in a food mill or electric blender.

Heat vegetable oil and sauté the remaining onion, which has been thinly sliced, until golden. Put in the ground-spice paste and fry for several minutes. Add lamb cubes and fry for 5 minutes. Add yogurt, salt, and water. Mix thoroughly. Cover and simmer until meat is tender.

If fresh coriander leaves are not available, substitute ¼ cup parsley and ¼ cup chives.

Lamb and Green Peas in Coconut Milk

2 medium onions, chopped	2 tablespoons grated unsweetened coconut
4 tablespoons vegetable oil	
4 cloves garlic, crushed	1 tablespoon poppy seeds, crushed
½ teaspoon grated ginger	
1 teaspoon salt	1 teaspoon cumin
2 pounds lamb, cubed	2-inch stick of cinnamon
4 bay leaves	6 cloves
1 cup water	4 cardamoms, crushed
1½ cups thick coconut milk	½ teaspoon turmeric
1 cup yogurt	½ teaspoon cayenne pepper
2 tablespoons slivered blanched almonds	1 cup green peas
	1 teaspoon sugar
2 tablespoons pistachio nuts	2 tablespoons vinegar
⅓ cup dried apricots, diced	3 hard-cooked eggs, quartered

Heat 2 tablespoons of the oil and fry onions until brown. Stir in garlic, ginger, salt and lamb cubes, and allow to brown. Add bay leaves and water. Cover and simmer about 45 minutes. Meanwhile, combine coconut milk, yogurt, almonds, pistachios and apricots. Set aside. In the remaining 2 tablespoons of oil, fry the coconut, poppy seeds, cumin, cinnamon, cloves, turmeric and cayenne pepper.

When the meat is cooked and only a little gravy remains, remove bay leaves and add fried spices and coconut milk mixture, stirring well to mix thoroughly. Continue cooking, keeping heat very low and watching carefully to prevent burning. Add peas. When mixture is well blended and peas are tender, remove from heat and stir in sugar and vinegar. Serve garnished with the hard-cooked eggs.

Masala Lamb Shanks with Green Beans

4 lamb shanks
2 large onions, chopped
4 tablespoons vegetable oil
6 cloves garlic, crushed
1 tablespoon grated ginger
3-inch stick of cinnamon
½ teaspoon black pepper
3 cloves
1½ teaspoons salt
½ teaspoon turmeric
radishes and green onions

2 fresh or pickled green chilies, chopped
2 tablespoons chopped coriander leaves, optional
3 tablespoons grated unsweetened coconut
2 cups water
1 pound green beans, cooked and drained
juice of 1 lemon

Brown onions and lamb shanks in oil. Add garlic, ginger, cinnamon, black pepper, cloves, salt, turmeric, green chilies, coriander leaves and coconut. Continue frying for several minutes and add water. Cover and simmer for about 2 hours or until tender. Mix in the cooked green beans. Add lemon juice, stirring well. Serve immediately, accompanied by radishes and green onions.

Lamb with Spinach

3 tablespoons vegetable oil	½ teaspoon turmeric
2 large onions, thinly sliced	¼ teaspoon cayenne pepper
1 tablespoon grated ginger	1½ pounds leg of lamb, cubed
4 cloves garlic, crushed	½ cup boiling water
2 teaspoons green pepper, minced	1 teaspoon salt
1 teaspoon cumin	2 large bunches spinach, washed and chopped

Brown onion in vegetable oil. Add ginger, garlic, green pepper, cumin, turmeric, and cayenne pepper. Fry for 2 or 3 minutes. Put in lamb cubes and fry for 5 minutes. Add boiling water and salt. Cover and simmer until meat is tender. Add chopped spinach. Cook until spinach is almost a puree.

Indian Style Lamb Cutlets

1 pound ground lamb	¼ teaspoon turmeric
2 fresh or pickled green chilies, chopped	½ teaspoon ground coriander
1 medium onion, finely chopped	1 teaspoon salt
	½ cup mashed potatoes
3 cloves garlic, crushed	3 eggs
1 teaspoon grated ginger	fine bread crumbs
	4 tablespoons vegetable oil

Combine lamb, green chilies, onion, garlic, ginger, turmeric, coriander, salt, mashed potatoes and 1 egg. Mix well and shape into small cutlets. Beat remaining 2 eggs. Dip each cutlet into bread crumbs, then in egg. Fry in the hot oil. Keep sprinkling a little of the beaten egg on each cutlet as they cook.

Lamb Bafat

3 tablespoons vegetable oil	3-inch stick of cinnamon
1 large onion, chopped	4 cloves
1 teaspoon grated ginger	3 cardamoms, crushed
6 cloves garlic, crushed	1 teaspoon salt
1 pound lean lamb, cubed	3 medium tomatoes, chopped
1½ cups hot water	3 medium potatoes, peeled and
¼ teaspoon chili powder	halved
½ teaspoon cumin	¼ cup vinegar
¼ teaspoon black pepper	2 teaspoons brown sugar

Sauté onion, ginger and garlic in 2 tablespoons of the vegetable oil. Put in meat cubes and brown them. Add hot water. Cover and simmer for about 30 minutes. Meanwhile, fry the chili powder, cumin, black pepper, cinnamon, cloves and cardamom in remaining tablespoon of oil. Add spice mixture, salt, tomatoes, potatoes and vinegar to the simmering meat. Continue cooking until meat and potatoes are tender. Just before serving, add brown sugar.

Spicy Fried Liver

1 teaspoon turmeric	1 pound calves liver
1 teaspoon grated ginger	3 tablespoons vegetable oil
2 cloves garlic, crushed	2 medium-sized onions, thinly
¼ teaspoon cayenne pepper	sliced
¼ teaspoon black pepper	juice of ½ lemon
1 tablespoon vinegar	1 teaspoon salt

Combine turmeric, ginger, garlic, cayenne pepper, black pepper, and vinegar.

Wash and pat dry the liver. Rub with spice paste. Heat vegetable oil and fry onions until golden. Put in liver and fry until browned. Sprinkle with lemon juice and salt just before serving.

Liver Curry

3 tablespoons vegetable oil
2 large onions, thinly sliced
2 cloves garlic, crushed
1 fresh or pickled green chili, finely chopped
¼ teaspoon ginger, finely chopped
2 teaspoons ground coriander
1 teaspoon paprika
½ teaspoon cumin
¼ teaspoon crushed black pepper
pinch of turmeric
1½ pounds calves liver, cut in 2-inch squares
1 teaspoon salt
1 cup thick coconut milk
juice of ½ lemon

Heat vegetable oil and brown the onions. Add garlic, green chili, ginger, coriander, paprika, cumin, black pepper and turmeric. Fry for 2 or 3 minutes. Put in liver squares and fry for 3 minutes, stirring constantly. Add salt and coconut milk. Simmer, uncovered about 10 minutes. Stir in lemon juice just before serving.

Pork Vindaloo

2 large onions	8 cloves
2 teaspoons mustard seeds	¼ teaspoon peppercorns
1 teaspoon cumin	½ cup cider vinegar
1 teaspoon turmeric	2 pounds pork loin, cubed
1 teaspoon cayenne pepper, or to taste	3 tablespoons clarified butter
1½-inch piece of ginger	2 large tomatoes, peeled and chopped
6 cloves garlic	2 bay leaves
1½-inch stick of cinnamon	2 teaspoons salt

In a food mill or electric blender, grind together the onions, mustard seeds, cumin, turmeric, cayenne pepper, ginger, garlic, cinnamon, cloves, peppercorns and vinegar. Mix with the pork cubes. Marinate at least 24 hours in a glass dish in the refrigerator.

When ready to cook, melt the butter in a heavy casserole. Add pork and marinade, tomatoes, bay leaves and salt. Cover and simmer about 2 hours, stirring frequently.

This dish is a Goanese specialty and should be very hot and sour.

Spicy Kababs

⅔ cup yogurt	¼ teaspoon crushed black pepper
1 tablespoon ground coriander	1 medium onion, finely chopped
2 teaspoons grated ginger	juice of 1 lime
½ teaspoon cayenne pepper	2 pounds lamb or beef, cubed
¼ teaspoon ground cloves	salt to taste
¼ teaspoon ground cinnamon	melted clarified butter
¼ teaspoon turmeric	

Combine yogurt, coriander, ginger, cayenne pepper, cloves, cinnamon, turmeric, black pepper, onion, lime juice, and meat cubes. Marinate at least 1 hour. Thread on skewers. Brush with melted butter and sprinkle with salt. Broil or grill until done.

Shami Kababs

1¼ pounds ground lamb or beef	1 teaspoon ground coriander
¼ cup yellow split peas, soaked for 1 hour	½ teaspoon cayenne pepper
	½ teaspoon cumin
1 cup water	⅛ teaspoon ground cinnamon
1 small onion	⅛ teaspoon turmeric
2 cloves garlic	1½ teaspoons salt
2 teaspoons chopped green pepper	1 teaspoon lime juice
	1 egg, beaten
1-inch piece of ginger	¼ cup vegetable oil
	raw onion slices
fresh coriander leaves, optional	

Combine ground lamb or beef, soaked split peas and water in a saucepan and cook uncovered until water has evaporated. Cool. Be sure there is very little excess fat in this mixture.

Grind together the meat mixture, onion, garlic, green pepper and ginger. Then grind again. Combine with the ground coriander, cayenne pepper, cumin, cinnamon, turmeric, salt, lime juice and beaten egg. Mix thoroughly and shape into small even-sized balls. Flatten and fry until brown in vegetable oil.

Serve garnished with raw onion slices and coriander leaves.

Seekh Kababs

1 pound ground lamb or beef
1 small onion, grated
2 cloves garlic, crushed
2 teaspoons ground coriander
¼ teaspoon cumin
⅛ teaspoon ground cloves

pinch of ground cardamom
pinch of powdered dry mustard
1 teaspoon salt
1 egg, beaten
2 to 3 tablespoons vegetable oil
   or clarified butter, melted
lime wedges

Combine ground meat, onion, garlic, coriander, cumin, cloves, cardamom, mustard, salt and egg. Mix thoroughly. Shape into 6 to 8 even-sized balls. Grease broiler pan and put in balls. Brush with vegetable oil or melted butter and broil until evenly browned. Serve with wedges of lime.

Cumin Kababs

1 pound ground lamb or beef
4 teaspoons cumin
1 teaspoon cayenne pepper
2 tablespoons finely chopped
   coriander leaves

1 small onion, grated
1 teaspoon salt
1 egg, beaten
¼ cup vegetable oil or melted
   clarified butter

Combine all ingredients except oil or butter. Mix well and shape like sausages. Heat oil or butter and fry until brown.

Note: You may substitute 1 tablespoon parsley and 1 tablespoon chives for coriander leaves.

Liver Kababs

1½ pounds thickly sliced calves' liver
2 teaspoons ground coriander
½ teaspoon grated ginger
1 clove garlic, crushed

¼ teaspoon ground cinnamon
¼ teaspoon black pepper
¼ teaspoon ground cloves
½ cup yogurt
melted clarified butter

salt

Wash liver. Pat dry with paper towels and cut into 1½-inch squares.

Combine liver with the coriander, grated ginger, garlic, cinnamon, black pepper, cloves, and yogurt. Set aside to marinate at least 1 hour.

Thread on skewers. Brush with melted butter and broil to desired doneness. Sprinkle with salt.

Kathi Kababs

2 pounds leg of lamb, cubed
2 medium onions, finely chopped
1 teaspoon crushed pepper
3 teaspoons cumin
8 cardamoms, crushed
½ teaspoon chili powder

1 teaspoon freshly grated ginger
2 teaspoons salt
unseasoned meat tenderizer, optional
¼ cup vegetable oil
1 lime, sliced
1 medium onion, thinly sliced

Place lamb cubes, chopped onion, and spices in mixing bowl and marinate for several hours. Meat tenderizer can be added if desired, according to package directions. String on skewers and brush with oil. Broil 7 to 10 minutes, or according to taste. Serve garnished with sliced lime and onion.

South Indian Chicken Curry with Cashew Nuts

4 tablespoons vegetable oil
1 fryer, 2½ to 3 pounds, disjointed
1 medium onion, finely chopped
1 teaspoon ground coriander
½ teaspoon turmeric
½ teaspoon cayenne pepper
⅛ teaspoon ground cinnamon
⅛ teaspoon ground cloves
½ teaspoon ginger, grated
pinch of ground cardamom

2 cloves garlic, crushed
2 teaspoons green pepper, chopped
½ cup grated unsweetened coconut
1 teaspoon salt
1 cup yogurt
1 cup water
⅔ cup cashew nuts
1 tablespoon butter
juice of 1 lime
mint leaves

Heat vegetable oil and brown the chicken parts. Remove and set aside. Fry onion until golden in remaining oil. Put in coriander, turmeric, cayenne pepper, cinnamon, cloves, ginger, cardamom, and garlic. Fry for 2 or 3 minutes. Stir in the green pepper, coconut, salt, yogurt, and water. Add browned chicken parts, cover and simmer until chicken is tender.

Meanwhile, sauté cashew nuts in butter. When chicken is done, stir in nuts and lime juice. Serve garnished with mint leaves.

Indian Fried Chicken I

½ teaspoon paprika
¼ teaspoon turmeric
¼ teaspoon cayenne pepper
¼ teaspoon black pepper
⅛ teaspoon ground cinnamon

1 teaspoon salt
1 frying chicken, 2½ pounds, disjointed
¼ cup vegetable oil or clarified butter

Combine paprika, turmeric, cayenne pepper, black pepper, cinnamon and salt. Rub this mixture into the chicken parts. Heat oil or butter and sauté the chicken until very tender.

Indian Fried Chicken II

3 tablespoons grated unsweetened coconut
1 medium onion, grated
1 tablespoon green pepper, minced
3 cloves garlic, crushed
½ teaspoon mint leaves, finely chopped
2 teaspoons ground coriander
½ teaspoon turmeric

¼ teaspoon cayenne pepper
pinch of ground cinnamon
pinch of ground cloves
2 tablespoons coriander leaves, chopped, optional
1 teaspoon salt, or to taste
1 fryer, 2½ to 3 pounds, disjointed
3 to 4 tablespoons vegetable oil
¼ cup water

Combine coconut, onion, green pepper, garlic, mint leaves, ground coriander, turmeric, cayenne pepper, cinnamon, cloves, coriander leaves and salt. Rub this mixture into chicken parts and set aside for 1 hour.

Heat oil and fry chicken for about 10 minutes. Add water, cover, and continue to cook over low heat until chicken is very tender, watching to see that it does not stick to bottom of pan.

Spiced Baked Chicken Indian Style

1 roasting chicken, 3 to 4 pounds, with giblets	1 teaspoon cumin
½ teaspoon salt	¼ teaspoon cayenne pepper
6 tablespoons vegetable oil or melted clarified butter	½ teaspoon grated ginger
1½ teaspoons ground coriander	3 tablespoons lemon pulp
1 teaspoon mustard seeds, crushed	½ teaspoon salt
	5 large onions, sliced
	4 medium potatoes, peeled and halved

butter

Stuffing:

2 whole cardamoms	1 teaspoon turmeric
1 fresh or pickled green chili	½ cup grated unsweetened coconut
6 cloves	3 tablespoons coriander leaves, optional
½-inch piece ginger	
3 cloves garlic	

In a food mill or electric blender, grind together the cardamoms, green chili, cloves, ginger, garlic, turmeric, coconut and coriander leaves.

Chop the chicken giblets and sauté in 2 tablespoons of the vegetable oil or butter for 5 minutes. Put in the spice paste and fry for several minutes. Rub inside of chicken with ½ teaspoon salt and stuff with fried spices and giblets. Truss.

Combine ground coriander, mustard seeds, cumin, cayenne pepper, grated ginger, lemon pulp and salt. Rub this over the chicken. (If any extra remains, it can be used between onions and potatoes, in the next step.)

In a large heavy casserole, put in the remaining 4 table-spoons of oil or melted butter. Spread half of the onion slices over the bottom. Put in chicken and surround with potatoes.

Spread remaining onions over potatoes. Dot top with butter. Cover tightly and seal edges with flour-and-water dough or with aluminum foil. Heat on top of stove until you begin to hear ingredients sizzling. Then place in a 350° oven for 1 hour and 20 minutes.

Chicken Pepper Curry

1½ teaspoons black pepper
½ teaspoon turmeric
¼ teaspoon salt
1 fryer, 2 to 2½ pounds, disjointed
4 tablespoons vegetable oil

3 medium onions, sliced
1 teaspoon green pepper, minced
½ teaspoon salt
½ cup water
1 cup thick coconut milk
1 cup green peas

Combine black pepper, turmeric and salt. Rub into the chicken parts and set aside.

Heat vegetable oil and fry onions until golden brown. Put in chicken parts, green pepper and salt. Fry for 5 minutes. Add water, cover and simmer about 20 minutes. Uncover, add coconut milk, mixing thoroughly. Continue simmering, uncovered, until chicken is almost done. Add peas and cook until tender.

Spicy Chicken
(Murgh Masalum)

1 fryer, 2½ to 3 pounds, disjointed
1 large onion
4 cloves garlic
2 tablespoons ground coriander
2 teaspoons cumin
2 teaspoons turmeric
4 large tomatoes, chopped

¼ teaspoon cayenne pepper
3 whole cardamoms
6 cloves
1-inch piece of ginger
2-inch stick of cinnamon
¼ cup clarified butter
1 teaspoon salt

In a food mill or electric blender, grind together the onion, garlic, coriander, cumin, turmeric, cayenne pepper, cardamoms, cloves, ginger and cinnamon. Rub this paste into the chicken parts.

Heat the butter and sauté the chicken for 10 minutes. Add salt and tomatoes. Cover tightly and simmer until chicken is tender and sauce is very thick.

Mild Chicken Curry with Potatoes

½ cup grated unsweetened
coconut
3 tablespoons vegetable oil
2 medium onions, finely
chopped
2 teaspoons ground coriander
1 teaspoon cumin
1 teaspoon mustard seeds,
crushed

½ teaspoon turmeric
¼ teaspoon crushed red pepper
4 cloves garlic, crushed
1 fryer, 2½ pounds, disjointed
1 teaspoon salt
1 cup water
2 tablespoons lemon pulp
2 large potatoes, peeled and
quartered

Spread coconut out on a flat pan and toast in a moderate oven until golden brown. Cool.

Heat oil and brown onions. Add coriander, cumin, mustard seeds, turmeric, red pepper and garlic. Fry for 2 or 3 minutes and then put in the chicken. Fry for 5 minutes. Mix in the toasted coconut, water, salt and lemon pulp. Cover and simmer for about 25 to 30 minutes. Add potatoes and continue simmering until chicken and potatoes are tender.

Instead of potatoes, 4 medium carrots can be used. Scrape and cut them in 2-inch pieces.

Stuffed Spicy Chicken
(Stuffed Murgh Masalum)

1 roasting chicken, 3 to 4 pounds	3 cloves garlic, crushed
½ teaspoon salt	1 medium onion, grated
½ teaspoon black pepper	4 teaspoons ground coriander
3 hard-cooked eggs, chopped	2 teaspoons cumin
1 medium onion, sliced	1 teaspoon poppy seeds, crushed
2 tablespoons blanched sliced almonds	½ teaspoon turmeric
2 tablespoons raisins	½ teaspoon salt
6 tablespoons clarified butter	½ teaspoon cayenne pepper
¼ cup grated unsweetened coconut	pinch of ground cardamom
	pinch of ground cloves
	1½ cups yogurt

Rub the inside of the chicken with the ½ teaspoon salt and pepper. Combine the chopped egg, sliced onion, almonds and raisins. Stuff the chicken with this. Truss and rub the skin with 2 tablespoons of the clarified butter.

Combine the coconut, garlic, grated onion, coriander,

cumin, poppy seeds, turmeric, salt, cayenne pepper, cardamom and cloves. Mix well.

Heat the remaining 4 tablespoons of the clarified butter in a heavy casserole and fry the spice mixture for 2 or 3 minutes. Stir in the yogurt, and bring to a simmer. Lay chicken in casserole, spoon some of the yogurt over it, and cover tightly. Roast in a 325° oven for 1½ hours, turning and basting occasionally.

Chicken with Sweet Potatoes

1 fryer, 2 to 2½ pounds, disjointed	3 tablespoons vinegar
	4 cloves
4 tablespoons vegetable oil	2-inch stick of cinnamon
2 teaspoons cumin	2 teaspoons brown sugar
1 teaspoon turmeric	1½ teaspoons salt
1-inch piece of ginger	1½ cups water
2 cloves garlic	3 medium sweet potatoes, peeled and quartered
1 teaspoon paprika	
2 medium onions	

Heat vegetable oil and brown chicken parts. Remove and set aside.

Grind together in a food mill or electric blender, the cumin, turmeric, ginger, garlic, paprika, onions and vinegar. Add this spice-mixture to the vegetable oil in the skillet and fry for a minute or two. Add cloves and cinnamon. Continue frying for another minute.

Put in chicken, brown sugar, salt and water. Cover and cook over low heat for about 30 minutes. Add sweet potatoes and simmer until tender, stirring occasionally.

Tomato Chicken Curry

4 tablespoons vegetable oil	½ teaspoon turmeric
2 medium onions, thinly sliced	¼ teaspoon cayenne pepper
3 cloves garlic, crushed	1 fryer, 2½ pounds, disjointed
4 cloves	3 large tomatoes, chopped
1 tablespoon ground coriander	1 cup yogurt
1 teaspoon cumin	1 teaspoon salt
1 teaspoon grated ginger	½ cup water

Brown onions in the vegetable oil. Add garlic, cloves, coriander, cumin, ginger, turmeric and cayenne. Fry for 2 or 3 minutes. Put in chicken and fry another 2 or 3 minutes, coating with the spices. Add tomatoes. Simmer 5 minutes and then add yogurt, salt and water. Cover and simmer until chicken is tender, stirring occasionally.

Kerala Coastal Chicken Curry

4 tablespoons clarified butter	2 whole cardamoms, crushed
2 large onions, thinly sliced	1 bay leaf
¼ teaspoon mustard seeds	½ teaspoon ginger, finely chopped
1 tablespoon ground coriander	
¼ teaspoon black pepper	1 teaspoon salt
½ teaspoon turmeric	1 fryer, 2½ to 3 pounds, disjointed
¼ teaspoon crushed red pepper	
¼ teaspoon aniseed	¼ cup water
¼ teaspoon ground cloves	2 medium potatoes, peeled and quartered
¼ teaspoon ground cinnamon	
1½ cups thick coconut milk	

Fry one of the onions until lightly browned in 2 tablespoons of the butter. Add mustard seeds and fry until they pop. Put in other 2 tablespoons of butter, coriander, black pepper, turmeric, red pepper, aniseed, cloves, cinnamon, cardamoms, bay leaf, and ginger. Cook for a minute or two and then put in remaining onion and chicken. Fry for 5 minutes, watching to see that it does not burn. Sprinkle on salt, add water, and simmer 10 minutes. Add potatoes and coconut milk and simmer, uncovered, until chicken is tender and potatoes are done, stirring occasionally.

If available, 2 tablespoons of coconut oil can be used instead of 2 tablespoons of butter.

Chicken with Coconut Milk and Eggs

1 frying chicken, 2½ to 3 pounds, cut up	1 teaspoon salt
2 teaspoons grated ginger	2 cups thin coconut milk
4 tablespoons vegetable oil	4 hard-cooked eggs
3 cloves garlic, crushed	1 tablespoon lemon juice
4 fresh or pickled green chilies, finely chopped	1 cup hot, cooked peas
1 teaspoon cumin	½ pound small whole potatoes, cooked
2 tablespoons finely chopped almonds	2 medium tomatoes, quartered
1 tablespoon chopped coriander leaves, optional	1 tablespoon chopped almonds
	a few coriander leaves, optional

Combine chicken and ginger and let marinate 1 hour. Fry the garlic, green chilies, cumin, almonds and chopped coriander leaves in hot vegetable oil for 2 or 3 minutes. Put in chicken and sauté 5 minutes. Add salt and coconut milk. Cover and simmer about 1 hour. Add eggs and remove from heat. Stir in lemon juice. To serve: place on a flat dish and surround chicken with hot peas and potatoes. Garnish with tomatoes, chopped almonds and whole coriander leaves.

Chicken Baked with Spiced Yogurt

¼ cup almonds	1 cup chopped tomatoes
½ cup grated unsweetened coconut	generous pinch of saffron
2 cloves garlic	1 fryer, 2 to 3 pounds, disjointed
1-inch piece of ginger	¼ cup clarified butter
1 teaspoon chili powder	2 onions, thinly sliced
1 cup yogurt	1 teaspoon salt
juice of 1 lemon	coriander or mint leaves, optional

Grind together the almonds, coconut, garlic, ginger, and chili powder in a food mill or electric blender. Add this mixture to the yogurt, along with the lemon juice, chopped tomatoes, and saffron. Add the chicken parts to this mixture. Be sure that each piece is coated. Let marinate 1 or 2 hours.

In a heavy casserole, melt the butter and sauté the onions until brown. Put in the chicken and its marinade. Add salt. Cover, bring to a simmer and seal edges of casserole with aluminum foil.

Bake in a 325° oven about 1½ hours. Serve garnished with coriander or mint leaves, if desired.

Tandoori Chicken

1 frying chicken, 2½ to 3 pounds, quartered	1 teaspoon cumin
1 cup yogurt	½ teaspoon cayenne pepper
3 cloves garlic, crushed	¼ teaspoon powdered anise seed
1½ teaspoons freshly grated ginger	4 tablespoons melted butter or vegetable oil
¼ cup lime juice	thinly sliced onion rings
2 teaspoons ground coriander	wedges of lime

Combine yogurt, garlic, ginger, lime juice, coriander, cumin, cayenne, and anise. Marinate chicken in this mixture for at least 24 hours (48 hours is better) in refrigerator. Put chicken pieces on a greased rack in a baking pan and roast at 375°, occasionally basting with the butter or oil until tender. Serve garnished with thinly sliced onion and wedges of lime. The ideal accompaniment with this is *nan.*

Chicken with Coconut Slivers

3 tablespoons vegetable oil	⅛ teaspoon ground cloves
2 medium onions, thinly sliced	2-inch stick of cinnamon
¼ teaspoon ground cardamom	¼ teaspoon chili powder
1 teaspoon turmeric	1 fryer, 2 to 2½ pounds, disjointed
1 teaspoon ground coriander	¼ of a fresh coconut
1 teaspoon poppy seeds, crushed	1 teaspoon salt
½ teaspoon peppercorns, crushed	2 tablespoons vinegar
	1 cup water

Heat vegetable oil and fry the onions until brown. Put in the ground cardamom, turmeric, coriander, poppy seeds, pepper, cloves, cinnamon, and chili powder, and fry for 2 or 3 minutes. Add chicken and fry another minute or two. Cut coconut into very thin slivers, leaving brown rind on, if desired; and add to chicken, along with salt, vinegar, and water. Cover and simmer about 1 hour, stirring frequently.

Chicken Curry with Greens

5 tablespoons vegetable oil	¼ teaspoon cayenne pepper
2 medium onions, finely chopped	2 whole cardamoms
	4 cloves
3 cloves garlic, crushed	2-inch stick of cinnamon
2 teaspoons ground coriander	2½-pound fryer, disjointed
1 teaspoon poppy seeds, crushed	1 teaspoon salt
½ teaspoon fenugreek seed, crushed	1 cup thick coconut milk
	2 cups turnip greens, washed and chopped
½ teaspoon cumin	
¼ teaspoon turmeric	juice of 1 lemon

Fry onions in vegetable oil until golden. Add garlic, coriander, poppy seeds, fenugreek, cumin, turmeric, cayenne pepper, cardamoms, cloves and cinnamon. Fry for 3 minutes. Add chicken and salt. Cover pan and slowly cook for about 15 to 20 minutes, watching carefully. If it seems to be too dry, sprinkle some water over top. Stir frequently.

Mix in the coconut milk and chopped greens. Simmer, uncovered, until chicken is tender and greens done. Stir in lemon juice just before serving.

In India, *methi bhaji* (fenugreek leaves) are generally used for greens in this particular dish. Here, however, you can also use shredded lettuce or even broccoli as a substitute.

Spicy Chicken Curry

3 tablespoons vegetable oil
1 medium onion, thinly sliced
2 cloves garlic, crushed
2 tablespoons ground coriander
1 teaspoon turmeric
2 teaspoons cumin
½ teaspoon mustard seed, crushed

½ teaspoon grated ginger
1 teaspoon crushed red pepper
2-pound fryer, disjointed
1 teaspoon salt
¼ cup water
1 cup thick coconut milk
2 tablespoons lemon juice

Sauté onion and garlic in vegetable oil until golden. Add coriander, turmeric, cumin, mustard seed, ginger and red pepper. Fry for several minutes. Put in chicken and sauté for 5 minutes. Add salt and water. Cover and simmer 15 minutes. Uncover, stir in coconut milk and continue simmering, uncovered, until chicken is very tender. Remove from heat and stir in lemon juice.

Chicken with Green Peas

4 tablespoons clarified butter
2 medium onions, thinly sliced
1 fryer, 2 to 2½ pounds, disjointed
2 fresh or pickled green chilies, finely chopped
1 teaspoon cumin
2 cloves garlic, crushed
¼ teaspoon ginger, finely chopped
2 tablespoons lemon juice

⅛ teaspoon black pepper
1 teaspoon mint leaves, finely chopped
½ cup grated unsweetened coconut
2-inch stick of cinnamon
6 cloves
1 teaspoon salt
1½ cups water
1 cup green peas

Heat 2 tablespoons of the clarified butter and brown the

onions. Remove and set aside. Add remaining 2 tablespoons of butter to the skillet and put in the chicken. Brown. Add green chilies, cumin, garlic, ginger, black pepper, mint leaves, coconut, cinnamon, cloves and salt. Fry for several minutes, stirring well. Add browned onion and water. Cover and simmer until chicken is almost done. Add peas and cook until tender. Just before removing from heat, stir in lemon juice.

Vegetable oil can be used for butter, however, the flavor will be improved with butter.

Chicken with New Potatoes

1 frying chicken, 2½ to 3 pounds, cut up	4 tablespoons vegetable oil
1 clove garlic, crushed	1 cup hot water
½ teaspoon freshly grated ginger	1½ teaspoons salt
1 teaspoon ground coriander	½ teaspoon cumin
2 medium onions, chopped	24 very small, new potatoes
	black pepper, to taste
	chives

Combine chicken, garlic, ginger, and coriander. Set aside to marinate for an hour or so. Heat 2 tablespoons vegetable oil and fry onions for 5 minutes. Add chicken and brown. Pour in hot water and add salt. Cover and simmer until tender. Meanwhile, wash and scrape new potatoes. In remaining 2 tablespoons of oil, cook the potatoes, shaking the pan from time to time. During last 5 minutes, sprinkle cumin and black pepper over them. Combine potatoes and chicken and serve sprinkled with chives.

Note: Lamb can be substituted for the chicken.

Chicken Vindaloo

1 teaspoon cumin
1 teaspoon turmeric
1 tablespoon ground coriander
4 cloves garlic
1-inch piece of ginger
6 cloves
3 fresh or pickled green chilies
½ cup vinegar
2 large onions, thinly sliced

3 tablespoons vegetable oil
2 teaspoons salt
1 frying chicken, 2½ to 3
   pounds, cut up
3-inch stick of cinnamon
2 cups hot water
3 medium potatoes, parboiled,
   peeled and halved
4 hard-cooked eggs, halved

In electric blender, whirl together the cumin, turmeric, coriander, garlic, ginger, cloves, green chilies and vinegar. Heat oil and lightly brown onions. Add chicken, salt, stick of cinnamon, vinegar-spice mixture and hot water. Cover and simmer for about 1 hour. Add halved potatoes and hard-cooked eggs and heat through.

Spicy Duck Curry

3 tablespoons vegetable oil
1 onion, thinly sliced
2 cloves garlic, crushed
2 fresh or pickled green chilies,
finely chopped, or to taste
2 tablespoons ground coriander
1 teaspoon turmeric
½ teaspoon cumin

1 teaspoon cayenne pepper
1 teaspoon ginger, finely
   chopped
4-pound duck, disjointed
1 teaspoon salt
1 cup water
1 cup thick coconut milk
¼ cup lemon juice

Heat vegetable oil and sauté onion until golden. Add garlic, green chilies, coriander, turmeric, cumin, cayenne pepper and ginger. Fry for several minutes. Put in duck, salt and water. Cover and simmer until duck is quite tender. Skim off excess fat and add coconut milk. Simmer 10 minutes, uncovered. Remove from heat and stir in lemon juice.

Duck Korma

1 tablespoon ground coriander	2 cloves garlic, crushed
1 teaspoon cumin	4-pound duck, disjointed
1 teaspoon turmeric	2 tablespoons vegetable oil
¼ teaspoon black pepper	1 large onion, thinly sliced
1 teaspoon grated ginger	4 cloves
pinch of cayenne pepper	3 whole cardamoms, crushed
1 teaspoon salt	3-inch stick of cinnamon
pinch of saffron	juice of 1 lemon
2 cups yogurt	coriander or mint leaves,
1 medium tomato, chopped	optional

Combine ground coriander, cumin, turmeric, black pepper, ginger, cayenne pepper, salt, saffron, yogurt, tomato, crushed garlic and duck parts. Set aside for 1 hour to marinate.

Heat vegetable oil in a heavy casserole and fry the onion, cloves, cardamoms and cinnamon for several minutes. Put in duck and yogurt marinade, mixing well. Cover and cook over low heat, watching carefully until duck is tender. Stir in lemon juice before removing from heat. Garnish with coriander or mint leaves, if desired.

Pepper Fried Duck

4-pound duck, disjointed
1½ teaspoons crushed pepper
1 teaspoon turmeric
1 teaspoon salt
3 medium onions, thinly sliced

1 clove garlic, crushed
1 tablespoon vinegar
6 tablespoons vegetable oil
1 cup water

Combine crushed pepper, turmeric, salt, garlic and vinegar, and rub this mixture into the duck. Set aside for 1 hour.

Heat 4 tablespoons of the vegetable oil and sauté the duck for 15 to 20 minutes. Remove excess fat and add water. Cover tightly and simmer about 1 to 1½ hours.

Meanwhile, brown the onions in the remaining 2 tablespoons of oil and set aside.

To serve: skim off excess fat and garnish with browned onion.

Madras Duck Vindaloo

1 tablespoon ground coriander
1½ teaspoons turmeric
2 teaspoons cumin
½ teaspoon cayenne pepper or to taste
¼ teaspoon black pepper
¼ teaspoon ground cardamom
2 teaspoons ginger, grated
4 cloves garlic, crushed

1 duck, disjointed, 4 to 5 pounds
2 tablespoons vegetable oil
1 large onion, finely sliced
3-inch stick of cinnamon
6 cloves
3 bay leaves
1 cup vinegar
½ cup water
1½ teaspoon salt or to taste

Combine coriander, turmeric, cumin, cayenne pepper, black

pepper, cardamom, ginger and garlic. Rub this mixture into duck parts and marinate 6 to 8 hours at room temperature, or if climate is very hot, in the refrigerator.

Heat vegetable oil and fry onion until golden. Put in duck, cinnamon, cloves and bay leaves. Fry for 5 minutes. Add vinegar, water and salt. Cover tightly and simmer 1½ to 2 hours, watching carefully. Skim off excess fat before serving.

Baked Duck and Vegetables

1 teaspoon cumin	pinch of cloves
1 teaspoon ground mustard	1 tablespoon vinegar
½ teaspoon turmeric	1 tablespoon clarified butter
¼ teaspoon cayenne pepper	1 duck, 4 to 5 pounds, disjointed
½ teaspoon salt	4 medium onions, thinly sliced
¼ teaspoon black pepper, crushed	1 small head cabbage, sliced
½ teaspoon ginger, grated	1 cup carrot slices
1 clove garlic, crushed	2 large tomatoes, sliced
	¼ cup water
mint leaves, optional	

Combine cumin, mustard, turmeric, cayenne pepper, salt, black pepper, ginger, garlic and cloves. Rub into the duck parts and set aside for 15 minutes.

Melt butter in a large heavy casserole. Put in a layer of onions, duck, cabbage and carrots. Continue with layers until all are used. Top with tomato slices and salt to taste. Sprinkle on water. Cover tightly and seal edges of casserole with aluminum foil. Heat on top of stove until it begins to cook; then put in a 350° oven for 1½ to 2 hours.

Serve garnished with mint leaves, if desired.

Duck Buffado

2 tablespoons vegetable oil	6 cloves
2 large onions, quartered	½ teaspoon ginger, finely
1 duck, 4 to 5 pounds, disjointed	chopped
1 teaspoon turmeric	2½ cups water
1 teaspoon ground coriander	1 small head cabbage, quartered
1 small green pepper, quartered	3 medium potatoes, halved
2-inch stick of cinnamon	1 cup green peas
1 teaspoon salt	2 tablespoons vinegar

In a large heavy casserole, heat the oil. Sauté onions until golden. Put in duck, and sprinkle on the turmeric and coriander. Add the green pepper, cinnamon, salt, cloves, ginger and water.

Cover the casserole tightly and bake in a 350° oven for 1 hour. Skim off as much excess fat as possible. Add cabbage and potatoes. Cover and return to oven for another 45 minutes to 1 hour. When almost done, add peas. Stir in vinegar just before serving.

VII. FISH AND SEAFOOD

BOTH FRESH AND SALT WATER fish are eaten extensively throughout India, usually in the form of a curry or in a pulao. Shrimp are also plentiful and used in a variety of dishes as well as salted and dried for future use.

Bombloe fish are caught in vast numbers off the west coast of India. Although they are eaten fresh locally, the majority of them are dried and exported to the West as "Bombay

Duck" — a name resulting from the fact that such large numbers are found swimming near the surface especially in the coastal area around Bombay. Bombay duck are considered by many to be a gourmet item, when thoroughly washed and fried in oil until light brown.

Among the most popular fish in India are *pomfret, beckti, sanghara* and *seer,* for which our best substitutes in the United States would be sole, flounder, cod and halibut.

Fish Curry Bengal Style

1 pound halibut, sea bass or cod	¼ teaspoon mustard seeds
	⅛ teaspoon ground cinnamon
1 teaspoon paprika	⅛ teaspoon ground cloves
⅛ teaspoon turmeric	⅛ teaspoon ground cardamom
salt	⅛ teaspoon turmeric
3 tablespoons vegetable oil	3 large tomatoes, chopped
3 large onions, finely chopped	1 tablespoon coriander leaves, chopped, optional
2 cloves garlic, crushed	
¼ teaspoon chili powder	¼ cup water
¼ teaspoon cumin	1½ teaspoons salt
½ cup yogurt	

Cut fish into serving pieces. Rub with paprika and turmeric; salt lightly. Heat oil and brown fish. Remove and set aside.

Fry onions and garlic until brown, adding more oil, if necessary. Add chili powder, cumin, mustard seeds, cinnamon, cloves, cardamom and turmeric. Fry for a minute or two. Put in tomatoes, coriander leaves and water. Simmer until tomatoes are tender. Add salt and yogurt. Put in fish, cover and simmer for about 10 minutes, watching carefully.

Use mustard oil, if available.

Fish with Tomato Yogurt Sauce

1 pound fillets, halibut or
    flounder
3 tablespoons vegetable oil
1 small onion, finely chopped
1 clove garlic, crushed
1 tablespoon coriander leaves,
    optional
1 fresh or pickled green chili,
    finely chopped

1 teaspoon ground coriander
⅛ teaspoon turmeric
¼ cup grated unsweetened
    coconut
¼ cup tomato sauce
1 cup yogurt
1 teaspoon salt or to taste

Lightly brown fish fillets in hot oil; remove from skillet and set aside. Put in onion and fry until golden. Add garlic, coriander leaves, green chili, coriander, turmeric and coconut. Fry for 2 or 3 minutes, stirring constantly. Add tomato sauce, yogurt and salt. Simmer for 5 minutes.

Put in fish, cover and simmer for five minutes, watching carefully.

Fish Kalia

4 to 6 tablespoons vegetable oil
1 pound fillets, cod or sea bass
1 large potato, cut into 1-inch
    cubes
1 cup cauliflower, cut up
2 medium onions, thinly sliced
1 teaspoon grated ginger
2 cardamoms, crushed slightly

2 cloves
1 clove garlic, crushed
¼ teaspoon turmeric
pinch of ground cinnamon
¼ teaspoon cayenne pepper
½ cup green peas
1½ teaspoons salt
⅔ cup yogurt
water

Heat 3 tablespoons of the oil and quickly brown fish pieces. Remove from skillet and set aside. Brown potatoes and cauliflower, adding more oil as necessary. Remove and set aside.

Brown onions. Add grated ginger, cardamoms, cloves, garlic, turmeric, cinnamon and cayenne pepper. Fry for 2 or 3 minutes. Add green peas, browned potato and cauliflower. Put in salt and yogurt. Simmer for a minute or two. Then add enough water to cook vegetables. When they are almost done, put in fish and simmer until done. Serve very hot.

Spicy and Sour Fish Curry

3 tablespoons vegetable oil	1 teaspoon turmeric
2 medium onions, very finely chopped	¼ teaspoon ground cardamom
	½ cup lemon juice
1 teaspoon ginger, finely chopped	1 teaspoon brown sugar
	1 cup yogurt
2 teaspoons ground coriander	1½ teaspoons salt
1 teaspoon cumin	1 pound fillets, cod, halibut or sea bass
½ teaspoon cayenne pepper or to taste	

Cook onion in vegetable oil until golden. Add ginger, coriander, cumin, cayenne, turmeric and cardamom, and fry for 2 or 3 minutes.

Stir in the lemon juice, brown sugar, yogurt and salt. Put in the fish which has been patted dry, cover, and simmer until done, stirring gently, occasionally.

Coastal Fish Curry

1 pound sole fillets	1 bay leaf, crumbled
1 teaspoon paprika	¼ teaspoon mustard seeds
1 teaspoon salt	1 fresh or pickled green chili,
4 tablespoons vegetable oil	finely chopped
2 medium onions, thinly sliced	⅛ teaspoon cloves
½ teaspoon grated ginger	1½ cups thick coconut milk
1 tablespoon white vinegar	

Dry fish between paper towels and cut into 2½-inch pieces. Combine paprika and salt. Rub this mixture into the fish. Heat the oil and fry fish until lightly browned. Remove and set aside.

Add the sliced onions to pan and fry until brown. Add ginger, bay leaf, mustard seeds, green chili and cloves, and fry for 2 or 3 minutes. Add coconut milk and fish. Simmer about 10 minutes. Remove from heat and stir in vinegar.

Fish with Yogurt
(Dahimachi)

2 medium onions, thinly sliced	¼ teaspoon ground cardamom
2 tablespoons vegetable oil	¼ teaspoon turmeric
1 teaspoon cumin	2 slices ginger, minced
¼ teaspoon ground cloves	1 pound halibut
¼ teaspoon ground cinnamon	1½ teaspoons salt
1½ cups yogurt	

Cut fish into serving pieces.

Heat oil and brown the onions. Add cumin, cloves, cinnamon, cardamom, turmeric and ginger. Fry for 2 or 3 minutes.

Put in fish, salt and yogurt. Mix well and simmer until fish is cooked, watching carefully and stirring occasionally.

If available, use mustard oil.

Fish Baked in Leaves
(Patrani Machhi)

½ coconut	½ teaspoon brown sugar
1 fresh or pickled green chili	juice of 1 large lime
1 teaspoon cumin	1 pound fish fillets, sole or
1 clove garlic	flounder
2 tablespoons coriander leaves, optional	large lettuce leaves
	3 tablespoons melted, clarified
1½ teaspoons salt	butter
1 teaspoon white vinegar	

In a food mill or electric blender combine the coconut, green chili, cumin, garlic, coriander leaves, salt, brown sugar and lime juice. Grind to a paste.

Cut the fish into serving portions and pat dry with paper towels. Coat them with the coconut paste and wrap in the lettuce leaves. Place in a greased casserole in one layer. Pour melted butter over top; then sprinkle with the vinegar.

Bake in a 375° oven for 45 to 55 minutes, until the lettuce is wilted and browned. Serve very hot.

Note: In India, banana leaves are used for the wrapping. If you happen to have any growing in your locality, do use them. Cabbage leaves can also be used.

Kerala Style Fried Fish

1 pound fish fillets, halibut or flounder	⅛ teaspoon crushed black pepper
1 tablespoon lemon juice	1 clove garlic, crushed
1 teaspoon chili powder	1 teaspoon salt
1 teaspoon turmeric	3 tablespoons coconut oil

Rub fish with lemon juice. Dry thoroughly with paper towels.

Combine chili powder, turmeric, crushed black pepper, garlic and salt. Rub into fish and let marinate for 1 hour.

Heat oil in skillet and fry fish until brown.

If coconut oil is not available, use clarified butter or vegetable oil.

Fish with Tomatoes

1 teaspoon cumin	1 teaspoon grated ginger
1 teaspoon paprika	1 large onion, grated
½ teaspoon turmeric	1 pound halibut
¼ teaspoon cayenne pepper	3 tablespoons vegetable oil
1½ teaspoons salt	1 tablespoon green pepper, finely chopped
2 cloves garlic, crushed	
4 large tomatoes, chopped	

Dry fish between paper towels and cut into strips 1½ inches by 3 inches. Combine cumin, paprika, turmeric, cayenne pepper, salt, garlic, ginger and onion. Rub this mixture into the fish strips and set aside for 1 hour to marinate.

Heat vegetable oil and fry the fish for several minutes. Remove fish. Add the green pepper and chopped tomatoes. Simmer until tomatoes have cooked to a puree. Add fish and heat thoroughly.

Curried Fish

3 tablespoons vegetable oil
1 small onion, finely chopped
2 cloves garlic, crushed
¼ teaspoon grated ginger
2 teaspoons ground coriander
¼ teaspoon cayenne pepper
½ teaspoon cumin
¼ teaspoon turmeric

⅛ teaspoon aniseed
pinch of cinnamon
pinch of black pepper
1 bay leaf, crumbled
1 pound fillets, halibut or sea
    bass
1 teaspoon salt
1 cup thin coconut milk

2 tablespoons white vinegar

Heat oil and brown onion. Add garlic, ginger, coriander, cayenne pepper, cumin, turmeric, aniseed, cinnamon, black pepper and the bay leaf. Fry for a minute or two. Put in fish and mix with spices. Add salt and coconut milk. Simmer until fish is cooked. Remove from heat and add vinegar.

Fried Spiced Fish

1 pound sole fillets
2 tablespoons lemon juice
½ teaspoon grated ginger
1 clove garlic, crushed
¼ teaspoon cumin

½ teaspoon paprika
½ teaspoon chili powder
¼ teaspoon turmeric
1½ teaspoons salt
vegetable oil for frying

Sprinkle lemon juice over fish. Dry with paper towels.

Combine ginger, garlic, cumin, paprika, chili powder, turmeric and salt. Rub this mixture into fish fillets and set aside for 1 hour to marinate.

Heat enough oil to cover the bottom of a skillet. Quickly sauté until nicely browned. Serve hot.

Tomato Fish Curry

1 pound snapper, sea bass or cod
1½ teaspoons salt
pinch of turmeric
2 tablespoons vegetable oil
1 small onion, chopped
1 teaspoon cumin
½ teaspoon cayenne pepper or to taste
1 teaspoon turmeric
2 teaspoons ground coriander
⅔ cup grated unsweetened coconut
2 teaspoons green pepper, finely chopped
2 large tomatoes, chopped
¾ cup water
1 bay leaf, crumbled
3 tablespoons lemon juice

Cut fish into serving slices and rub well with salt and pinch of turmeric.

Heat oil and fry onion until golden brown. Put in the cumin, cayenne pepper, turmeric and ground coriander, and fry for 2 or 3 minutes. Add coconut and green pepper. Stir for a minute or two. Put in tomato and water. Mix well. When sauce comes to a boil, add fish, bay leaf and lemon juice. Lower heat, and simmer until fish is tender.

Malayalee Fish Pappas

2 tablespoons coconut oil
1 large onion, chopped
2 tablespoons ground coriander
¼ teaspoon cumin
¼ teaspoon chili powder
¼ teaspoon turmeric
1 fresh or pickled green chili, finely chopped
¼ teaspoon ginger, finely chopped
1½ teaspoons salt
¼ cup water
1 pound halibut, sea bass or snapper
1 cup thick coconut milk
3 tablespoons white vinegar

Heat oil and brown the onion. Add coriander, cumin, chili powder, turmeric, green chili and ginger. Fry for a minute or two. Add water and salt, stirring thoroughly. Put in fish and simmer for 5 minutes. Add coconut milk and simmer until fish is very tender. Remove from heat and stir in the vinegar.

If coconut oil is not available, use clarified butter or vegetable oil.

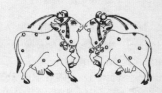

Spiced Fried Fish

1 pound fish fillets — cod, sea bass or halibut	1 teaspoon cumin
1 teaspoon salt	1 teaspoon cayenne pepper or to taste
¼ teaspoon turmeric	2 cloves garlic
2 medium onions	3 tablespoons vegetable oil
1 teaspoon mustard seed	2 tablespoons water

Rub fish with salt and turmeric. Set aside.

Grind together one of the onions, mustard seed, cumin, cayenne pepper and garlic in a food mill or electric blender.

Heat vegetable oil. Fry the remaining onion which has been finely chopped. When onion is brown, put in fish and fry for several minutes. Add the ground onion-spice paste, mixing well to coat the fish. Sprinkle in the water. Cover and simmer until fish is very tender.

Baked Fish
Malayalee Style

1½ pounds fish fillets—sea bass, cod or snapper
1 teaspoon chili powder or to taste
aluminum foil
1 teaspoon aniseed, crushed
1 teaspoon salt
2 tablespoons white vinegar
1 tablespoon melted butter

Combine chili powder, aniseed and salt. Rub into fish fillets. Place fillets side by side on a large sheet of aluminum foil. Pour on vinegar and melted butter.

Fold up the foil and seal edges securely. Place on a cookie sheet and bake in 400° oven about 45 minutes.

In Kerala banana leaves are used for the wrapping.

Fish with Coconut Milk

2 tablespoons vegetable oil
1 small onion, thinly sliced
⅛ teaspoon turmeric
1 clove garlic, crushed
½ teaspoon grated ginger
1 teaspoon green pepper, finely chopped
juice of 2 limes
½ teaspoon crushed red pepper
1 pound cod, halibut or snapper
1½ teaspoons salt
2 tablespoons water
2 medium potatoes, cooked and quartered
1 cup thick coconut milk

Heat vegetable oil and sauté onion until golden. Add turmeric, garlic, ginger, green pepper and crushed red pepper. Fry 2 or 3 minutes. Put in fish which has been cut into serving pieces; salt it and sprinkle on water. Cook about 5 minutes.

Add potatoes and coconut milk. Simmer until fish is tender, watching carefully. Remove from heat and add lime juice. Serve hot.

Parsi Fish Sas

1 teaspoon chili powder or to taste
1 teaspoon cumin, ground
1 clove garlic, crushed
½ teaspoon salt
1 pound fish fillets, cod or halibut

3 tablespoons vegetable oil
1 medium onion, chopped
½ cup vinegar
1½ tcaspoons sugar
2 eggs, beaten

Combine chili powder, cumin, garlic and salt and rub into fish. Set aside for 1 hour. Heat oil and lightly sauté onion. Add fish and continue cooking until fish is flaky. Meanwhile, combine vinegar, sugar and eggs. Pour this mixture over fish, watching carefully. Heat gently for several minutes. The sauce must not boil or it will curdle.

Spicy Shrimp

2 pounds raw shrimp, shelled
and deveined
1 teaspoon salt
1 teaspoon crushed red pepper
or to taste
1 teaspoon turmeric

1 teaspoon ground cumin
2 teaspoons ground coriander
2 cloves garlic, crushed
4 tablespoons vegetable oil
juice from 2 lemons
2 tablespoons chopped chives

Combine shrimp, salt, crushed red pepper, turmeric, cumin, coriander and garlic. Let stand 1 hour. Heat oil, add spiced shrimp and cook until tender and done. Just before serving add lemon juice and chives.

Spiced Shrimp with Potatoes

3 large potatoes, cubed
6 tablespoons vegetable oil
2 pounds raw shrimp, shelled
and deveined
1 teaspoon chili powder or to
taste

2 cloves garlic, crushed
2 teaspoons ground cumin
½ teaspoon turmeric
¾ teaspoon salt
2 fresh or pickled green chilies,
chopped

1 tablespoon finely chopped fresh coriander leaves, optional

Heat 3 tablespoons oil and sauté potatoes until half done. Drain and reserve. Combine shrimp, chili powder, garlic, cumin, turmeric and salt. Add remaining oil and shrimp to pan. Sauté for several minutes. Add potatoes and continue cooking until done. Serve garnished with chopped green chilies and fresh coriander leaves.

Shrimp Patia

2 pounds raw shrimp, shelled
    and deveined
½ teaspoon salt
½ teaspoon turmeric
1 teaspoon cayenne pepper or
    to taste
4 tablespoons vegetable oil
2½ cups sliced onions
½ teaspoon finely chopped
    fresh ginger

3 cloves garlic, crushed
2 fresh or pickled green chilies,
    chopped
1 teaspoon ground cumin
2 tomatoes, finely chopped
1 tablespoon fresh coriander
    leaves, chopped, optional
1 teaspoon brown sugar

Combine shrimp, salt, turmeric and cayenne pepper. Set aside. Heat oil and fry onions until golden. Add ginger, garlic, green chilies and cumin; fry 2 or 3 minutes. Add shrimp and cook until half done. Then add tomatoes and coriander leaves and cook until water from tomatoes has evaporated. Add brown sugar and serve. The usual accompaniment for this dish would be fried green chilies; however, fried green peppers could be substituted.

Shrimp Vindaloo

1 teaspoon cumin
1 teaspoon mustard seed
½-inch piece ginger
¼ teaspoon turmeric
2 cloves garlic
1 teaspoon cayenne pepper or
    to taste
2 medium onions
¼ cup white vinegar

2 pounds raw shrimp, shelled
    and deveined
3 tablespoons vegetable oil
1 teaspoon salt
½ cup water
2 large tomatoes, chopped
2 medium potatoes, cooked and
    quartered

Grind together the cumin, mustard seed, ginger, turmeric, garlic, cayenne pepper, one of the onions, and the vinegar in an electric blender. Combine with shrimp and set aside for 1 hour to marinate.

Heat vegetable oil and brown the remaining onion which has been thinly sliced. Put in shrimp-spice mixture and fry for 2 or 3 minutes. Add salt, water and tomatoes. Simmer 10 minutes. Add potatoes and simmer until heated through.

Shrimp Curry Goanese Style

3 tablespoons coconut oil
1 small onion, sliced
1 teaspoon chili powder or to taste
2 teaspoons ground coriander
¼ teaspoon turmeric
1 teaspoon cumin
4 cloves garlic, crushed
½ cup grated unsweetened coconut

½ teaspoon ginger, finely chopped
1 tablespoon green pepper, finely chopped
1½ teaspoons salt
juice and pulp of 2 lemons
¾ cups water
2 pounds raw shrimp, shelled and deveined

Brown onion in coconut oil. Add chili powder, ground coriander, turmeric, cumin, garlic, coconut and ginger. Fry 2 or 3 minutes. Put in green pepper, salt, juice and pulp of the lemons, and water. When it begins to simmer, add shrimp and cook until done.

If coconut oil is not available, use clarified butter.

Shrimp Curry with Coconut Milk

2 tablespoons vegetable oil
1 large onion, finely chopped
¼ teaspoon turmeric
¼ teaspoon grated ginger
¼ teaspoon ground cinnamon
¼ teaspoon ground cloves
¼ teaspoon ground cardamom
1 teaspoon salt
1 cup thick coconut milk
2 pounds shrimp, boiled and
    peeled

Heat oil and fry onion until golden. Add turmeric, ginger, cinnamon, cloves, cardamom and salt. Fry for 2 or 3 minutes. Gradually stir in coconut milk. Simmer, uncovered, for 10 minutes. Add shrimp and simmer 5 minutes.

Shrimp and Okra Patia

3 medium onions, thinly sliced
4 tablespoons vegetable oil
4 cloves garlic, crushed
1 teaspoon cayenne pepper or
    to taste
1 teaspoon cumin
½ teaspoon ground coriander
1 teaspoon turmeric
1 pound okra, cut up
1 pound raw shrimp, peeled
    and deveined
1 teaspoon salt
½ cup tomato paste
1 tablespoon brown sugar
½ cup hot water
3 tablespoons lemon juice

Fry onions in vegetable oil until lightly browned. Add garlic, cayenne pepper, cumin, coriander and turmeric, frying and stirring for several minutes. Add cut-up okra and continue cooking for a few more minutes. Put in shrimp, salt, tomato paste, brown sugar and hot water. Simmer about 10 minutes. Stir in lemon juice.

Mild Shrimp Curry

1 pound raw shrimp, peeled and deveined	2 tablespoons grated unsweetened coconut
½ teaspoon chili powder	1 teaspoon salt
3 cloves garlic, crushed	3 medium tomatoes, peeled and chopped
½ teaspoon cumin	1 cup boiling water
1½ teaspoons ground coriander	1 tablespoon lemon juice
¼ teaspoon turmeric	

Combine chili powder, garlic, cumin, coriander, turmeric, coconut, salt, tomatoes and hot water. Bring to a boil and simmer for 10 minutes. Add shrimp and cook till done. Add lemon juice.

Shrimp Curry

2 medium onions, finely chopped	1 teaspoon chili powder
2 tablespoons vegetable oil	½ teaspoon grated fresh ginger
3 cloves garlic, crushed	½ cup grated unsweetened coconut
4 teaspoons ground coriander	2 cups hot water
1 small green pepper, finely chopped	1 teaspoon salt
½ teaspoon cumin	1½ pounds raw shrimp, shelled and deveined
½ teaspoon turmeric	juice of 1 lemon

Sauté onions in oil until golden. Add garlic, coriander, green pepper, cumin, turmeric, chili powder, ginger and coconut. Fry 5 minutes. Put in boiling water and simmer 10 minutes. Add shrimp, salt them, and cook until done. Add lemon juice.

Hot Shrimp Curry with Coconut

2 tablespoons vegetable oil
1 medium onion, finely chopped
1 tablespoon ground coriander
1 teaspoon cumin
1½ teaspoons cayenne pepper
½ teaspoon mustard seeds, crushed
⅛ teaspoon black pepper, crushed

1 bay leaf, crumbled
2 cloves garlic, crushed
⅔ cups grated unsweetened coconut
¼ cup lemon juice
1½ teaspoon salt
1 cup water
2 pounds raw shrimp, shelled and deveined

Heat oil and fry onion, coriander, cumin, cayenne pepper, mustard seed, black pepper, bay leaf and garlic for 2 or 3 minutes. Put in coconut and fry another minute or two. Add lemon juice, salt and water. Simmer 10 minutes. Add shrimp and cook until done.

Crab Curry

3 tablespoons vegetable oil
2 medium onions, chopped
2 teaspoons ground coriander
½ teaspoon chili powder
¼ teaspoon cumin
¼ teaspoon turmeric
1 clove garlic, crushed
½ teaspoon grated ginger

pinch of cinnamon
¾ cup grated unsweetened coconut
2 large tomatoes, chopped
1 teaspoon salt
1 cup water
1½ pounds crab meat
3 tablespoons lemon juice

Heat oil and fry onions until golden. Add coriander, chili powder, cumin, turmeric, garlic, ginger, cinnamon and coconut. Fry for 3 minutes. Add tomatoes, salt and water. Simmer about 15 minutes. Put in crab meat and continue simmering 10 to 12 minutes. Stir in lemon juice just before removing from heat.

VIII. VEGETABLES

SINCE A LARGE NUMBER of India's population are vegetarians, it is not surprising to find there some of the most delicious vegetable dishes in the entire world. Strictly speaking, a vegetarian is one who does not eat meat, fish or eggs. Fortunately, an infinite variety of vegetables are available in India, including most of those grown in the United States.

The Indians have raised the art of cooking vegetables to

soaring heights. There are endless ways to produce a truly unique dish, each one different and more tantalizing than the previous one. Even the humblest vegetable becomes a feast for a king in India.

The following recipes are only a few of the most popular Indian vegetable preparations which can transform a simple meal into a delightful taste-experience.

Spicy Eggplant

3 small eggplants	½ cup grated unsweetened coconut
6 tablespoons vegetable oil	
1 tablespoon ground coriander	juice and pulp of 2 lemons
1 teaspoon chili powder or to taste	1 teaspoon salt
	1 bay leaf
¼ teaspoon turmeric	1 teaspoon toasted sesame seeds, crushed
1 fresh or pickled green chili, finely chopped	
	1 cup water
3 large onions, thinly sliced	1 teaspoon mustard seeds
3 cloves garlic, crushed	1 teaspoon brown sugar
2 tablespoons coriander leaves, chopped	

Cut the eggplants in quarters lengthwise. Brown them in 4 tablespoons of the hot oil. Remove from skillet and set aside. In the remaining 2 tablespoons of oil, fry the coriander, chili powder, turmeric, green chili, onions and garlic for 5 minutes. Add coconut and fry another 2 or 3 minutes. Put in the lemon juice and pulp, salt, bay leaf, sesame seeds and water. Stir well. Add eggplant quarters. Cover and simmer until eggplant is very tender and sauce is thickened. Add brown sugar and mustard seeds which have been fried in a little oil until they pop. Mix well and serve garnished with coriander leaves.

Eggplant Bhurta

2 medium eggplants	1 teaspoon cumin
3 tablespoons vegetable oil	½ teaspoon chili powder
2 medium onions, thinly sliced	¼ teaspoon turmeric
2 cloves garlic, crushed	1 teaspoon salt
⅔ cup yogurt	

Bake eggplants in a 350° oven for 45 to 50 minutes. Cool; peel and chop rather fine.

Heat oil and fry onion until brown. Add garlic, cumin, chili powder, turmeric and salt. Cook a few minutes and put in the eggplant. Continue cooking about 5 minutes, stirring well. Stir in yogurt and remove from heat.

Eggplant with Yogurt

1 large eggplant	1 teaspoon ground coriander
4 tablespoons vegetable oil	¼ teaspoon cayenne pepper
3 large onions, chopped	½ teaspoon turmeric
2 cloves garlic, crushed	1 teaspoon cumin
1 tablespoon freshly grated ginger	1 teaspoon salt
½ teaspoon sugar	1 cup yogurt

Roast eggplant for 1 hour in a 350° oven or until tender. When cool, peel and cut into cubes.

Brown onions in 2 tablespoons of the vegetable oil. Add garlic, ginger, coriander, cayenne, turmeric, cumin and salt. Fry for several minutes. Add other 2 tablespoons of the oil and the eggplant cubes. Cook about 5 minutes. Just before serving, stir in the yogurt and sugar. This is usually served with kitchri.

Stuffed Eggplant Indian Style

¼ cup vegetable oil	1 tablespoon lemon juice
2 tablespoons ground coriander	1 teaspoon salt
2 teaspoons cumin	3 small eggplants
1 teaspoon turmeric	1 teaspoon fenugreek seeds
½ teaspoon chili powder	1 teaspoon mustard seeds
½ cup grated unsweetened	2 medium onions, thinly sliced
coconut	1 bay leaf, crumbled
1 cup water	

Heat 2 tablespoons of the vegetable oil and fry the coriander, cumin, turmeric, chili powder and coconut for several minutes. Add lemon juice and salt.

Meanwhile, slit eggplant lengthwise about three-quarters of the way to the end (do not cut completely through). Stuff the spiced coconut mixture into the slits.

In a heatproof casserole, heat other 2 tablespoons of oil and fry fenugreek and mustard seeds until they pop. Put in the onions and fry until golden brown. Add bay leaf and any of the remaining spiced coconut mixture. Put in the stuffed eggplants and water. Cover and simmer slowly until tender.

Eggplant Curry

2 medium onions, chopped
4 tablespoons vegetable oil
3 cloves garlic, crushed
2 tablespoons green pepper, finely chopped
½ teaspoon grated fresh ginger
1 teaspoon salt

½ teaspoon chili powder, or to taste
½ teaspoon turmeric
1 large eggplant, cut in 1-inch cubes
3 large tomatoes, chopped

Sauté onions in hot oil until golden. Add garlic, green pepper, ginger, chili powder and turmeric. Fry for 2 or 3 minutes. Put in eggplant cubes and fry for several minutes, stirring constantly. Add a little water and simmer 5 minutes. Add tomatoes and salt. Cover and simmer over very low heat about 10 minutes, stirring occasionally.

Eggplant in Coconut Milk

1 large eggplant, sliced
1 teaspoon turmeric
1½ teaspoons salt
5 tablespoons vegetable oil
½ teaspoon mustard seeds
1 small onion, chopped
1 clove garlic, crushed
1 fresh or pickled green chili, finely chopped
½ teaspoon sugar

1 teaspoon grated ginger
2 teaspoons ground coriander
1 teaspoon cumin
½ teaspoon chili powder, or to taste
1 bay leaf
pinch of cinnamon
3 tablespoons vinegar
1½ cup thin coconut milk

Mix together salt and turmeric and rub into eggplant slices. Heat 4 tablespoons of the vegetable oil and brown the eggplant slices (in a Teflon pan, if possible). Remove from skillet and set aside.

Heat remaining tablespoon of oil and fry mustard seeds until they crackle. Put in onion, garlic, green chili, ginger, coriander, cumin, chili powder, bay leaf and cinnamon. Fry a minute or two. Meanwhile, add vinegar to eggplant slices and then combine with onion-spice mixture. Stir in coconut milk and simmer very slowly, stirring frequently, for about 15 to 20 minutes. Watch carefully, as this will burn very easily. Add sugar just before removing from the pan.

Kerala Theeyal

2 cups eggplant, cut in 1-inch cubes
3 tablespoons vegetable oil
¼ teaspoon turmeric
¼ teaspoon chili powder or to taste
½ cup grated, unsweetened coconut, toasted
¼ teaspoon black pepper, crushed
1 teaspoon salt
1 cup water
¼ cup lemon juice
1 small onion, finely chopped
1 tablespoon green pepper, finely chopped
⅛ teaspoon fenugreek seed
⅛ teaspoon mustard seed

Heat 2 tablespoons of vegetable oil and put in the eggplant cubes. Sprinkle on the turmeric and chili powder and fry for 2 or 3 minutes, stirring constantly.

Add the grated coconut, which has been toasted previously a golden brown in the oven, to the eggplant. Put in black pepper, salt and water. Mix well and simmer about 10 minutes.

Meanwhile, fry mustard and fenugreek seeds in the remaining tablespoon of oil until they pop. Put in the onion and brown. Add to the eggplant along with the lemon juice. Stir thoroughly and simmer another 5 minutes or until the eggplant is quite tender.

Lime Curry

4 limes	¼ teaspoon chili powder
boiling water	1 teaspoon cumin
2 tablespoons vegetable oil	1 teaspoon mustard seeds
1 medium onion, finely chopped	1 tablespoon ground coriander
	¼ teaspoon turmeric
1 fresh or pickled green chili, finely chopped	1 bay leaf, crumbled
	⅓ cup grated, unsweetened coconut
2 cloves garlic, crushed	
¼ teaspoon ginger, finely minced	1 teaspoon salt
	1 cup water

Wash limes and simmer for 5 minutes in boiling water — to remove the bitter taste. Drain and cut in small pieces.

Heat vegetable oil and fry onion, green chili and garlic for five minutes. Add ginger, chili powder, cumin, mustard seeds, coriander, turmeric, bay leaf and coconut. Fry for a minute or two. Add limes, salt and water. Cover and simmer for about 45 minutes, stirring occasionally.

Bengali Curried Vegetables

4 tablespoons vegetable oil
¼ teaspoon mustard seeds
¼ teaspoon fenugreek seeds
¼ teaspoon aniseeds, crushed
1 teaspoon cumin
pinch of cayenne pepper
1 small bay leaf, crumbled
1 teaspoon chopped green
pepper

2 medium potatoes, peeled and
diced
1 small eggplant, peeled and cut
in 1-inch cubes
1 cup pumpkin (or squash) cut
in 1-inch cubes, optional
1 cup green peas
1 teaspoon salt or to taste
½ teaspoon sugar

Heat oil and fry mustard seeds, fenugreek seeds, aniseeds, cumin, cayenne pepper and bay leaf for a minute or two. Put in green pepper, potatoes, eggplant, pumpkin and green peas. Stir and sauté for 5 minutes. Add salt, sugar and just enough water to cook vegetables. Cover and simmer until tender.

Avial

1 small eggplant, cut in 1-inch
cubes
1 small sweet potato, cut in
1-inch cubes
½ cup green peas
½ cup green beans
1 carrot, sliced
1 small onion, sliced
¼ cup green pepper, diced
1 tablespoon melted butter

⅛ teaspoon turmeric
⅛ teaspoon cumin
1½ cups water
1 teaspoon salt, or to taste
1 medium tomato, diced
pulp of 1 lemon, diced*
⅓ cup grated unsweetened
coconut
1 cup yogurt

* If available, use ½ of a green mango, diced, instead of the lemon pulp.

Combine eggplant, sweet potato, green peas, green beans, carrot, onion, green pepper, turmeric and cumin. Add water and salt and simmer until vegetables are well cooked and little water remains.

Add tomato, lemon pulp and coconut. Simmer 5 minutes. Remove from heat and stir in yogurt and butter.

This is a typical Kerala dish.

Indian Stuffed Green Peppers

6 tablespoons vegetable oil	pinch of asafetida, optional
1 small onion, finely chopped	1½ cups mashed potatoes
2 cloves garlic, crushed	½ cup sesame seeds, toasted
2 teaspoons grated ginger	and crushed
1 teaspoon cumin	1½ teaspoons salt
¼ teaspoon cayenne pepper or to taste	6 medium green peppers
	juice of 1 lemon
¼ teaspoon turmeric	water

Heat 2 tablespoons of the vegetable oil and fry the onion until lightly browned. Add garlic, ginger, cumin, cayenne pepper, turmeric and asafetida. Fry for 2 or 3 minutes; then combine with the mashed potatoes, toasted crushed sesame seeds and salt. Set aside.

Cut a slit in the side of each pepper and remove seeds. Stuff with the seasoned mashed potato mixture. Heat the remaining vegetable oil in a skillet large enough to hold peppers in a single layer. Put in peppers and let fry for 5 minutes. Sprinkle with the lemon juice, cover and cook until tender, occasionally sprinkling on a little water, if necessary. Serve with yogurt.

Bean Sprouts
(Titori)

2 tablespoons vegetable oil	¼ teaspoon turmeric
2 medium onions, chopped	½ teaspoon grated fresh ginger
½ teaspoon cumin	1 clove garlic, crushed
1 tablespoon grated unsweet-	½ teaspoon salt
ened coconut	1 pound bean sprouts
1 cup thin coconut milk	

Sauté onions in vegetable oil until golden. Add cumin, coconut, turmeric, ginger, garlic and salt. Fry for 2 or 3 minutes. Add bean sprouts and coconut milk. Simmer about 7 to 10 minutes. Serve with *chappatis*.

Potato Korma

1 medium onion, finely chopped	1½ pounds small potatoes, peeled and sliced
3 tablespoons vegetable oil	4 tablespoons grated unsweet- ened coconut
½ teaspoon caraway seeds	¼ cup water
¼ teaspoon chopped fresh ginger	1½ cups yogurt
4 cloves	1 tablespoon chopped cori- ander leaves
1 clove garlic, crushed	
pinch of ground cinnamon	1 tablespoon chopped mint leaves
pinch of cardamom	
1 teaspoon salt	2 fresh or pickled green chilies, chopped
crushed red pepper, to taste	

In hot oil sauté onion until golden. Add caraway seeds, fresh ginger, cloves, garlic, cinnamon, cardamom, salt and red pepper. Cook for several minutes. Put in potatoes and grated coconut. Stir thoroughly and fry about 5 minutes. Add water, cover and simmer until potatoes are tender. Add yogurt and heat thoroughly. Serve garnished with green chilies, coriander and mint leaves.

Dahi Potatoes

1 tablespoon vegetable oil	1 teaspoon salt or to taste
2 fresh or pickled green chilies, finely chopped	1 cup yogurt
1 clove garlic, crushed	16 small new potatoes, boiled in their jackets
¼ teaspoon turmeric	

Heat oil. Put in green chilies, garlic and turmeric. Fry for several minutes. Stir in yogurt and salt. When heated through, put in potatoes and simmer until thoroughly heated.

Potato Bhurta

2 tablespoons vegetable oil	½ teaspoon turmeric
½ teaspoon mustard seeds	½ teaspoon chili powder
1 small onion, chopped	1½ teaspoons salt
1 teaspoon green pepper, finely minced	2 cups hot mashed potatoes
	1 tablespoon lime juice
1 tablespoon chopped coriander leaves	

Heat oil and fry mustard seeds until they pop. Add onion and green pepper and fry until lightly browned. Add turmeric, chili powder and salt. Fry for 1 minute. Add potatoes and lime juice. Mix well. Garnish with coriander leaves. Serve with pooris.

Potatoes in Yogurt

2 medium onions, chopped   ⅔ cup yogurt
2 tablespoons vegetable oil   2 teaspoons ground coriander
½ teaspoon cumin   ½ teaspoon chili powder
¼ teaspoon turmeric   1 teaspoon salt
        3 medium potatoes, cooked and diced

Heat the vegetable oil and brown the onions. Add the cumin, turmeric, and coriander; fry for another minute. Combine the yogurt, chili powder and salt; add to the fried onions. Put in potatoes and simmer slowly for 10 minutes.

Potatoes with Onions and Tomatoes

2 medium onions, thinly sliced   ½ teaspoon grated ginger
3 medium potatoes, peeled and   3 tablespoons vegetable oil
              quartered   ½ teaspoon turmeric
1 teaspoon fresh or pickled   2 medium tomatoes, chopped
green chili, finely chopped   1 teaspoon salt
        ¼ teaspoon mustard seeds

Sauté the onions, potatoes, green chilies and ginger in hot oil for 5 minutes. Add turmeric and stir. Put in tomatoes and salt. Simmer until potatoes are tender. Add a little water occasionally — enough to cook the potatoes and form a thick sauce. Just before serving, fry mustard seeds in a little oil for a minute or two and stir into potatoes. Excellent served with pooris.

Potato and Pea Curry
(Aloo Matar)

3 tablespoons vegetable oil	pinch of ground cloves
1 medium onion, finely chopped	pinch of ground cinnamon
½ teaspoon cumin	2 tablespoons tomato paste
½ teaspoon turmeric	½ cup boiling water
¼ teaspoon chili powder	3 medium potatoes, cooked and quartered
1 teaspoon grated ginger	1½ cups half-cooked peas
pinch of ground cardamom	1 teaspoon salt or to taste
½ cup yogurt	

Fry onion in vegetable oil until lightly browned. Add cumin, turmeric, chili powder, grated ginger, cardamom, cloves and cinnamon. Fry for 2 or 3 minutes. Put in tomato paste and boiling water. Mix well. Add potatoes, peas and salt. Simmer until peas are tender. Add yogurt and mix well.

Potatoes and Spinach
(Aloo Palak)

3 medium potatoes, peeled and
quartered
4 tablespoons vegetable oil
2 cloves garlic, crushed
¼ teaspoon cayenne pepper, or
to taste

1 teaspoon grated ginger
1 tablespoon chopped coriander
leaves, optional
1 teaspoon salt
1 pound spinach, washed and
chopped

Heat vegetable oil and brown the potato quarters. Put in
garlic, cayenne pepper, ginger, coriander leaves and salt. Fry
for several minutes. Add spinach. Cover and cook slowly
until spinach and potatoes are tender. A little water can be
added if it gets too dry before it is done.

Spicy Potatoes and Coconut

4 tablespoons clarified butter
2 teaspoons ground coriander
½ teaspoon chili powder
½ teaspoon turmeric
½ teaspoon cumin
4 medium potatoes, cooked,
peeled and cubed

½ cup grated unsweetened
coconut
juice and pulp of 1 lemon
1 teaspoon salt
¼ cup water (about)
¼ teaspoon fenugreek seeds
1 medium onion, finely chopped

Heat 3 tablespoons of the clarified butter in a skillet. Add
ground coriander, chili powder, turmeric and cumin. Fry for
2 or 3 minutes. Add potatoes, coconut, lemon juice and pulp,
and salt. Mix well. Add water — enough to keep mixture

from burning. Simmer very slowly for about 5 minutes. Meanwhile, heat remaining tablespoon of clarified butter. Fry fenugreek seeds for a minute, then add onion and brown it. Stir into potatoes and serve.

Potatoes with Tomatoes

½ teaspoon mustard seeds	1 teaspoon turmeric
3 tablespoons vegetable oil	¼ teaspoon grated ginger
3 large potatoes, cooked, peeled and diced	pinch of cayenne
	1 teaspoon salt
3 medium tomatoes, finely diced	½ teaspoon sugar
	1 teaspoon chopped coriander leaves, optional
2 teaspoons minced green pepper	

Fry mustard seeds in hot oil. Add diced potatoes and fry 5 minutes. Add tomatoes, green pepper, turmeric, grated ginger, cayenne, salt, sugar and coriander leaves. Cook slowly until tomatoes are done. Remove from fire and serve hot.

Curried Potato Balls

Potato Balls:

2 cups hot mashed potatoes	½ teaspoon salt
2 tablespoons onion, finely minced	2 eggs
	1 tablespoon flour
⅛ teaspoon chili powder	deep fat

Sauce:

1 tablespoon vegetable oil	⅛ teaspoon turmeric
1 small onion, finely chopped	¼ teaspoon cumin
2 teaspoons ground coriander	3 large tomatoes, chopped
½ teaspoon chili powder or to taste	1 cup water
	1 teaspoon salt
¼ cup yogurt	

Combine hot mashed potatoes, onion, chili powder, salt, eggs and flour. Mix well and drop by the spoonful into hot fat. When browned, drain well and keep warm.

Heat vegetable oil and fry onion, coriander, chili powder, turmeric and cumin for 2 or 3 minutes. Put in tomatoes, water and salt. Simmer about 15 minutes. Stir in yogurt. Add potato balls and serve very hot.

Cauliflower Curry

1 teaspoon grated ginger	3 tablespoons vegetable oil
2 cloves garlic, crushed	1 teaspoon cumin
1 teaspoon salt	¼ teaspoon ground cardamom
¼ teaspoon black pepper	⅛ teaspoon ground cinnamon
1 cup yogurt	⅛ teaspoon ground cloves
1 medium cauliflower, cut in flowerets	¼ teaspoon cayenne pepper, optional
3 medium onions, thinly sliced	¾ cup water

Combine ginger, garlic, salt, black pepper and yogurt. Add these to the cauliflower, mixing well.

Fry the onions in vegetable oil until lightly browned. Put in the cumin, cardamom, cinnamon, cloves and cayenne pepper, if desired. Fry for 2 or 3 minutes. Add cauliflower-yogurt mixture and fry very slowly for several minutes. Add water, cover and simmer slowly until tender.

Cauliflower with Peas and Tomatoes

1 small onion, finely chopped	3 large tomatoes, peeled and
2 tablespoons vegetable oil	chopped
¼ teaspoon chili powder	1 teaspoon salt
½ teaspoon turmeric	½ bay leaf, crumbled
1 teaspoon ground coriander	¼ cup water
2 cups cauliflower flowerets	1 tablespoon chopped coriander
1 cup green peas	leaves, optional

Fry onion in oil until golden. Add chili powder, turmeric and coriander. Fry for a few minutes. Put in cauliflower and peas and fry several minutes. Add tomatoes, salt, bay leaf and water. Cover and simmer until vegetables are tender. Garnish with chopped coriander leaves.

Cauliflower Bhujjia

½ teaspoon mustard seeds	1 teaspoon turmeric
1 tablespoon vegetable oil	pinch of cayenne pepper, or to
1 small onion, finely chopped	taste
2 cloves garlic, crushed	1 teaspoon salt
¼ teaspoon ginger, finely	1 medium cauliflower, cut up
slivered	¼ cup water
1 teaspoon lemon juice	

Heat oil and fry mustard seeds until they crackle. Put in onion, garlic, ginger, turmeric and cayenne. Fry for 5 minutes. Add cauliflower pieces and salt. Stir for a minute or two. Add water and cover. Cook until cauliflower is tender. Sprinkle with lemon juice.

Cauliflower with Yogurt

1 teaspoon vegetable oil	½ teaspoon chili powder
¼ teaspoon cumin	¼ teaspoon turmeric
¼ teaspoon mustard seeds	1 teaspoon salt
1 medium cauliflower, divided	¼ cup water
into flowerets	¼ cup yogurt

Heat oil and add cumin and mustard seeds. When they pop, add cauliflower, chili powder, turmeric, salt and water. Cover and cook until tender. Add yogurt just before removing from fire.

Cauliflower with Raisins

2 tablespoons vegetable oil	3 tablespoons raisins
½ teaspoon mustard seeds	1 teaspoon salt
1 teaspoon cumin	water
½ teaspoon ginger, finely	½ teaspoon sugar
chopped	1 teaspoon lime juice
1 medium cauliflower, divided	
into flowerets	

Heat oil and fry cumin and mustard seeds until they pop.

Add ginger and fry for another minute. Put in cauliflower, raisins and salt. Sauté for several minutes. Add enough water to cook cauliflower. Cook until tender. Add sugar and lime juice. Mix well.

Cauliflower and Potatoes North Indian Style

3 tablespoons vegetable oil
2 teaspoons ground coriander
¼ teaspoon chili powder
¼ teaspoon turmeric
1 tablespoon green pepper, finely chopped
1 medium onion, thinly sliced

1 medium cauliflower, divided into flowerets
2 medium potatoes, peeled and quartered
1 teaspoon salt
pinch of black pepper
water

1 tablespoon lemon juice

Fry coriander, chili powder and turmeric in hot oil. Put in green pepper and onion and sauté for a minute or two. Mix in cauliflower, potatoes, salt and black pepper. Add just enough water to cook vegetables. Cover and cook till tender and water has evaporated. Sprinkle with lemon juice.

Cabbage Foogath

2 tablespoons vegetable oil
¼ teaspoon mustard seeds
1 small onion, finely chopped
½ teaspoon cumin
¼ teaspoon turmeric
pinch of chili powder, optional

1 teaspoon salt
3 cups cabbage, shredded
½ cup water
¼ cup grated unsweetened
  coconut

Heat oil and fry mustard seeds until they crackle. Add onion and fry till golden. Put in cumin and turmeric. Then add salt and cabbage. Sprinkle on water; cook till tender, stirring frequently. Add grated coconut and chili powder and cook another minute or two.

Spicy Cabbage

3 tablespoons vegetable oil
¼ teaspoon mustard seeds
1 small onion, chopped
1 fresh or pickled green chili,
  finely chopped
¼ teaspoon turmeric

¼ teaspoon chili powder
4 cups cabbage, shredded
1 teaspoon salt or to taste
2 teaspoons chopped chives
¾ cup water
juice of 1 lime

Heat oil and fry mustard seeds until they pop. Put in onion and fry until light brown. Add green chili, turmeric and chili powder, and fry for a minute. Mix in cabbage, salt and chives; fry for 3 minutes, stirring well. Add water and simmer about 7 minutes. Add lime juice and mix thoroughly.

Pumpkin and Yogurt
(Erisheri)

2 cups pumpkin, cut into
¾-inch squares
1½ teaspoons salt
2 tablespoons vegetable oil
1½ teaspoons yellow split peas,
soaked for 1 hour and drained

1 bay leaf, crumbled
1 teaspoon ground dry mustard
2 tablespoons grated unsweetened coconut
¾ cup yogurt

Combine pumpkin and salt. Add enough water to cook. Simmer until tender and drain.

Heat vegetable oil and fry split peas until browned, sprinkling in the bay leaf during last minute of cooking. Add to yogurt. Combine mustard and coconut and add to the yogurt mixture, along with the drained pumpkin. Mix well. Add more salt if necessary.

Mixed Vegetable Curry

3 tablespoons vegetable oil
2 teaspoons ground coriander
½ teaspoon chili powder
¼ teaspoon turmeric
¼ teaspoon ginger, chopped
finely
2 cloves garlic, crushed
3 tablespoons grated unsweetened coconut
1 cup cauliflower, cut up

2 small potatoes, peeled and
quartered
1 cup green peas
1 large carrot, sliced
1 medium onion, thinly sliced
2 large tomatoes, chopped
1 fresh or pickled green chili,
finely chopped
¼ cup water
1 teaspoon salt or to taste
¼ cup lemon juice

Heat vegetable oil and fry coriander, chili powder, turmeric, ginger, garlic and coconut for 2 or 3 minutes. Add cauliflower, potatoes, green peas and carrot. Fry for 5 minutes. Put in onion, tomatoes, green chili, salt and water. Simmer until all the vegetables are tender, adding a little more water if it gets too dry. Add lemon juice, simmer a few more minutes.

Spicy Mixed Vegetable Curry

1 cup shredded cabbage	¼ teaspoon ground cardamom
1 cup green peas	⅛ teaspoon ground cinnamon
1 cup green beans, sliced	⅛ teaspoon ground cloves
2 medium potatoes, peeled and diced	¼ teaspoon chili powder, optional
3 tablespoons vegetable oil	½ teaspoon ginger, finely chopped
2 medium onions, thinly sliced	2 tablespoons coriander leaves, chopped
1 teaspoon green pepper, chopped	1 teaspoon salt or to taste
1 tablespoon ground coriander	1½ cups thick coconut milk
½ teaspoon cumin	juice of ½ lemon
½ teaspoon aniseed, crushed	

Combine cabbage, green peas, green beans and potatoes. Add just enough water to cook without burning and simmer for 5 minutes. Drain.

Meanwhile, heat vegetable oil and fry onions until golden. Add green pepper, ground coriander, cumin, aniseed, cardamom, cinnamon, cloves, chili powder, ginger and coriander leaves. Fry for a minute or two. Put in mixed vegetables and salt. Fry for several minutes, stirring frequently; and then put in coconut milk. Simmer gently until vegetables are tender, watching carefully to prevent burning. Remove from heat and add lemon juice.

Mixed Vegetables in Tomato Sauce

2 teaspoons ground coriander
1 teaspoon mustard seeds
½ teaspoon cumin
½ teaspoon turmeric
1 teaspoon paprika
¼ teaspoon cayenne pepper
2 cloves garlic
½-inch piece of ginger
2 large onions
3 tablespoons vegetable oil

1 cup cauliflower, cut up
1 cup squash, cut in 1-inch cubes
1 cup green beans, sliced
1 cup green peas
1½ teaspoons salt or to taste
1 cup tomato sauce
¾ cup water
1 tablespoon chopped mint leaves, or 1 tablespoon parsley

Grind together in a food mill or electric blender, the coriander, mustard seeds, cumin, turmeric, paprika, cayenne pepper, garlic, ginger and one of the onions.

Chop the other onion and fry it in the vegetable oil until lightly browned. Add the spiced-onion paste and fry for 2 or 3 minutes. Add cauliflower, squash, green beans and green peas. Fry an additional 2 or 3 minutes. Add salt, tomato sauce and water. Simmer until vegetables are tender. Serve garnished with mint or parsley.

South Indian Vegetable Moilee

2 tablespoons vegetable oil	2 medium potatoes, cut in
2 medium onions, thinly sliced	1-inch cubes
1 teaspoon turmeric	2 carrots, sliced
2 cloves garlic, crushed	½ cup green beans, sliced
½ teaspoon ginger, finely	½ cup green peas
chopped	1 teaspoon salt
1 bay leaf, crumbled	2 tablespoons water
1 fresh or pickled green chili,	1 cup thick coconut milk
finely chopped	juice of 1 large lime

Fry onion in vegetable oil until golden. Add turmeric, garlic, ginger, bay leaf and green chili, and fry for a minute or two. Put in potatoes, carrots, green beans, peas and salt. Continue frying about 5 minutes. Sprinkle in the water and cook until it has evaporated. Add coconut milk and simmer very slowly until vegetables are done, watching carefully. Remove from heat and add lime juice.

Spinach with Yogurt

2 bunches spinach	½ teaspoon cumin
2 tablespoons vegetable oil	¼ teaspoon sugar
1 medium onion, chopped	¼ teaspoon chili powder
1 clove garlic, crushed	½ teaspoon salt
¼ teaspoon turmeric	1 cup yogurt
1 hard-cooked egg, chopped	

Wash and clean spinach. Cook until tender and drain well. Cut up with 2 knives or chop very fine. Fry onion in oil until lightly browned. Add garlic, turmeric, cumin, sugar, chili powder and salt. Continue frying for several minutes. Add spinach and yogurt. Stir well. Heat through. Serve garnished with chopped hard-cooked egg.

Spiced Spinach Puree
(Palak Sag)

2 large bunches spinach	1 teaspoon ginger, grated
2 tablespoons vegetable oil	chili powder to taste
2 medium onions, finely chopped	1 teaspoon salt

Wash and finely chop spinach. Heat oil and brown onions. Add ginger and chili powder and fry one minute. Put in spinach. Cover and cook until all the water has evaporated. Add salt. Mash and stir well. Serve hot.

Okra Sas

1 pound okra	1 fresh or pickled green chili, chopped
2 tablespoons vegetable oil	
2 medium onions, chopped	1 teaspoon salt
1 clove garlic, crushed	1½ cups hot water
¼ teaspoon ginger, finely chopped	3 eggs
	2 tablespoons vinegar
2 tablespoons chopped coriander leaves, optional	

Wash and slice okra into half-inch rounds. Fry onions in oil until golden. Add garlic, ginger and green chili, and fry another minute or two. Put in okra, salt and hot water and cook until okra is done. Beat eggs; mix in vinegar. Gently add this to okra, taking care not to boil. It is advisable to add the egg mixture with pan set off the direct heat and then let it wait a few minutes so that sauce will thicken. Garnish with chopped coriander leaves.

Stuffed Okra
(Stuffed Bhendi)

1 pound okra	½ teaspoon cayenne pepper, or
1 teaspoon ground coriander	to taste
1 teaspoon turmeric	juice of 1 lime
½ teaspoon salt	3 tablespoons vegetable oil

Wash okra and slit one side. Mix together the coriander, turmeric, salt and cayenne pepper. Stuff okra with this mixture. Heat oil and carefully put in okra. Sprinkle with lime juice. Cover and cook over low heat for about 20 minutes, occasionally shaking the pan to be sure that none are sticking.

Seasoned Okra
(Seasoned Bhendi)

1 pound okra	1 teaspoon cumin
½ teaspoon turmeric	¼ teaspoon cayenne pepper or
2 teaspoons ground coriander	to taste
1 teaspoon salt	3 tablespoons vegetable oil

Slice okra into small pieces. Heat oil and add spices. Fry

for a minute or two. Add okra and cover. Stir occasionally, cooking over low heat until tender.

Squash
(Olan)

2 cups squash, cut into 1-inch cubes
1 cup lima or butter beans
1 teaspoon chopped green pepper
1 small onion, sliced
water

1 cup thick coconut milk
1 teaspoon cumin
1 teaspoon salt
¼ teaspoon chili powder, or to taste
pinch of black pepper
1 tablespoon butter

Combine squash, beans, green pepper and onion. Add just enough water to cover. Simmer until tender. Add coconut milk, cumin, salt, chili powder and black pepper. Mix well and bring to a boil. Add butter, stir and remove from heat.

Spicy Onions

3 medium onions, thinly sliced
3 tablespoons vegetable oil
½ teaspoon ginger, finely chopped
1 tablespoon lemon juice

½ teaspoon salt
1 teaspoon ground coriander
½ teaspoon turmeric
¼ teaspoon cumin

Heat oil. Put in onions, ginger, salt, ground coriander, turmeric and cumin. Fry slowly until very soft and tender. Add lemon juice and cook another 5 minutes.

Kerala Ginger Curry

½ cup fresh ginger, peeled and   ½ teaspoon mustard seeds
    cut into small pieces   ½ teaspoon fenugreek seeds
2 tablespoons salt   ½ teaspoon chili powder
water   ½ cup water
½ of a fresh coconut   ½ cup lemon juice
2 tablespoons vegetable oil   2 teaspoons brown sugar

Combine 1 tablespoon salt, ginger pieces and water to cover. Simmer 10 minutes. Drain. Repeat this process.

Peel off brown skin of coconut and cut into very fine pieces. Heat oil and fry coconut pieces until they begin to brown. Remove from pan and set aside. In the same oil fry mustard and fenugreek seeds until they crackle. Add chili powder, ginger pieces and fried coconut. Fry for a minute or two. Put in ½ cup water, lemon juice and brown sugar, and simmer until liquid is reduced to about ½ cup. Can be refrigerated for some time.

Cucumber Curry

2 tablespoons clarified butter   2 cups cucumber, peeled and
½ teaspoon mustard seeds   cut in large dice
1 small onion, finely chopped   1 cup water
1 clove garlic, crushed   juice and pulp of ½ lemon
¼ teaspoon chili powder   1 teaspoon salt or to taste
¼ teaspoon turmeric   ½ teaspoon sugar
3 tablespoons grated unsweet-
    ened coconut

Heat the clarified butter and fry mustard seeds until they

crackle. Add onion and cook until golden. Put in the garlic, chili powder and turmeric. Fry for 2 or 3 minutes. Add the coconut, cucumber, water, lemon juice and pulp, and salt. Simmer until cucumber is tender. Stir in the sugar.

Green Bean Foogath

2 tablespoons vegetable oil	2 cups sliced green beans,
¼ teaspoon mustard seeds	cooked
1 small onion, chopped	½ teaspoon salt
pinch of cayenne pepper	¼ cup grated unsweetened
½ bay leaf, crumbled	coconut

Heat oil and add mustard seeds. When they crackle, add onion and fry until golden. Add cayenne pepper and bay leaf. Cook for a minute, and then put in green beans, salt and coconut. Stir well. Simmer for about 5 minutes. A little water can be sprinkled on if mixture is too dry, during the last few minutes of cooking. Serve hot.

Fried Green Beans
Indian Style

1 pound green beans, cut up	1 small onion, finely chopped
boiling water	½ teaspoon chili powder
2 tablespoons vegetable oil	1 teaspoon salt or to taste
pinch of turmeric	

Cook beans in boiling salted water until barely tender. Drain.

Meanwhile, sauté onion in oil until brown. Add chili powder and turmeric. Then add beans and salt. Fry until moisture has evaporated and beans are cooked.

Kalan

3 medium bananas, moderately ripe
1 teaspoon turmeric
1 fresh or pickled green chili, finely chopped
¼ cup water
2 tablespoons vegetable oil
1 small onion, thinly sliced
½ teaspoon crushed black pepper

¼ teaspoon cumin
1 teaspoon mustard seed
½ teaspoon fenugreek seeds
2 cups yogurt
¼ cup grated unsweetened coconut
¾ teaspoon salt
pinch of cayenne pepper

Peel bananas and cut into 1-inch pieces. Combine them with turmeric and green chili. Add water and cook over moderate heat until bananas are very tender and water has been absorbed.

Fry onion in 1 tablespoon of vegetable oil until brown. Remove and set aside. Heat remaining tablespoon of oil and fry black pepper, cumin, mustard and fenugreek seeds until the seeds crackle. Add to yogurt along with coconut, salt and browned onion. Stir well.

Add bananas and a pinch of cayenne pepper to the seasoned yogurt. Mix well. Let stand several hours before serving so that flavors are well blended; serve at room temperature.

Tomato Bhurta

6 large tomatoes
1 tablespoon vegetable oil
1 medium onion, chopped
2 cloves garlic, crushed
1 fresh or pickled green chili,
    finely chopped

¼ teaspoon paprika
½ teaspoon cumin
1 teaspoon salt
1 tablespoon chopped coriander
    leaves, optional

Plunge tomatoes into boiling water for 2 to 3 minutes. Then peel and chop them.

Heat vegetable oil. Add onion, garlic, green chili, paprika and cumin. Fry until onion is browned. Add tomatoes and salt. Simmer 5 to 10 minutes. Serve garnished with coriander leaves.

In India the tomatoes would be roasted for about 10 minutes in hot ashes before being chopped.

Tomato and Onion Bhujjia

3 tablespoons vegetable oil
3 large onions, thinly sliced
1 fresh or pickled green chili,
    finely chopped
1 teaspoon cumin

¼ teaspoon paprika
1 teaspoon salt
4 large tomatoes, peeled and
    quartered

Heat oil and fry onions until lightly browned. Add green chili, cumin, paprika and salt; fry for two minutes. Add tomatoes and simmer very slowly about 15 minutes, stirring frequently to prevent scorching.

IX. SOUPS AND LENTILS

SOUPS ALONE have never played an important role in the
Indian meal. When served along with a dry curry, however,
and used to moisten rice, as we would use gravy, they become
a delicious accompaniment. These mixers are usually made
from a base of one of the many lentils, popularly known as
dhals, of which there are about fifty varieties in India.

Mulligatawny soup, as we know it in the western world, is

not typically Indian, although its concept originated in South India. The literal translation of "mulligatawny" is "pepper water" (*molliga* meaning pepper and *tunni* meaning water). The idea was taken over by the Anglo-Indians who began making it with meat and meat stock, and eventually the versions were multiplied further and adopted by Europeans. So the mulligatawny soup we think of in the United States is quite different from the South Indian mulligatawny or "pepper water."

Lentils, among the cheapest and commonest foods, are usually served with most Indian meals, especially in the North. They are consumed with great gusto by the rich and the poor alike, and are a very important item in the diet of India's vegetarians who number in the millions.

Sambhar

⅓ cup yellow split peas	¼ teaspoon turmeric
1 onion, thinly sliced	pinch of asafetida, optional
2 fresh or pickled green chilies, finely chopped	2 teaspoons salt
	⅓ medium green pepper, cut up
3½ cups boiling water	1 medium tomato, cut up
2 tablespoons vegetable oil	pinch of fenugreek seeds
1 tablespoon ground coriander	⅛ teaspoon mustard seeds
½ teaspoon chili powder	1 small onion, finely chopped
¼ teaspoon cumin	¼ cup lemon juice

Soak split peas 12 hours or overnight, then drain. Bring water to a boil and add peas, sliced onion and green chilies. Cover and simmer for 1 hour.

Heat 1 tablespoon of the vegetable oil and fry the coriander, chili powder, cumin, turmeric and asafetida for 2 or 3 minutes. Add to the simmering peas, along with the green pepper and tomato. Put in salt. Simmer ½ hour.

In remaining 1 tablespoon of oil, fry the fenugreek and mustard seeds until they crackle. Add onion and brown lightly. Add to the split peas. Stir in lemon juice. Serve with rice, idlis or dosais.

Coriander Rasam

3 tablespoons yellow split peas	¼ teaspoon cumin
4 cups water	¼ teaspoon turmeric
2 tablespoons vegetable oil	¼ teaspoon mustard seeds
1 small onion, finely chopped	½ teaspoon crushed red pepper
1 clove garlic, crushed	pinch of fenugreek seeds
1 bay leaf, crumbled	pinch of crushed black pepper
4 teaspoons ground coriander	2 tablespoons lemon juice
1½ teaspoons salt	

Boil the split peas in the water until soft.

Heat the vegetable oil and lightly fry the onion. Add the garlic, bay leaf, coriander, cumin, turmeric, mustard seeds, red pepper, fenugreek seeds and crushed black pepper. Fry for one or two minutes. Add to the boiled peas, along with the lemon juice and salt.

Simmer for 15 minutes. Strain and serve hot.

Tomato and Lime Rasam

¼ cup yellow split peas	1 bay leaf
4 cups water	1 tablespoon vegetable oil
2 large tomatoes, chopped	1 teaspoon mustard seeds
1 tablespoon chopped green pepper	¼ teaspoon cumin
	½ teaspoon chili powder
2 tablespoons chopped coriander leaves	pinch of asafetida, optional
	1½ teaspoons salt
3 tablespoons lime juice	

Boil the yellow peas in the water until tender. Strain, reserving both peas and liquid. Mash peas and set aside.

Add tomatoes, green pepper, coriander leaves and bay leaf to the liquid. Simmer 15 minutes.

Heat vegetable oil and fry the mustard seeds, cumin, chili powder and asafetida for a minute or two. Add to the soup, along with salt and the mashed peas. Simmer for 5 minutes. Remove from heat and stir in lime juice.

Substitute 1 tablespoon chopped parsley and 1 tablespoon chives for coriander leaves, if you wish.

Sukke Dhal

1 cup lentils	½ teaspoon chopped ginger
3 tablespoons vegetable oil	2 teaspoons ground coriander
1 medium onion, finely chopped	½ teaspoon crushed red pepper
	¼ teaspoon turmeric
3 cloves garlic, crushed	water
1 teaspoon salt	

Soak lentils for 1 hour and drain. Heat vegetable oil and fry the onion until golden brown. Add garlic, chopped ginger, coriander, red pepper and turmeric. Fry for 2 or 3 minutes. Put in the lentils and fry for 5 minutes. Add about 1 cup water, cover, and simmer over low heat until lentils are done, about 1 hour. More water can be sprinkled on, if it begins to stick. Most of the moisture should have evaporated when done. Add salt and stir well before serving.

Pepper Water

1 tablespoon ground coriander	¼ teaspoon crushed red pepper
½ teaspoon cumin seed, crushed	2 cups boiling water
	1 teaspoon salt
½ teaspoon mustard seeds, crushed	1 tablespoon vegetable oil
	1 small onion, thinly sliced
1 teaspoon peppercorns, crushed	2 cloves garlic, crushed
2 tablespoons lemon juice	

Combine coriander, cumin seed, mustard seed, peppercorns and crushed red pepper in a small dry skillet. Stir over moderate heat for 2 minutes. Do not let them burn. Add these spices to boiling water, along with salt, and simmer 10 minutes. Strain.

Meanwhile, gently sauté the onion and garlic in the vegetable oil until golden. Add to the strained liquid. Stir in the lemon juice and bring to a boil. Remove from heat and serve hot with rice.

In India this is used to moisten and flavor the rice when the curry that is served is a dry one.

Cumin Rasam

2 cloves garlic, crushed	4 cups water
1 teaspoon mustard seeds, crushed	1 teaspoon salt
	pinch of black pepper
1 medium onion, chopped	1 teaspoon brown sugar
2 tablespoons cumin seed	2 tablespoons lemon juice
¼ teaspoon turmeric	1 tablespoon vegetable oil

Lightly fry the garlic, mustard seeds, onion, cumin, and turmeric. Add this to the water along with salt, pepper, brown sugar and lemon juice. Mix well and simmer 15 to 20 minutes. Strain. Serve hot.

South Indian Cucumber Soup

2 tablespoons vegetable oil	¼ cup grated unsweetened coconut
1 small onion, finely chopped	
½ teaspoon cumin	1 cup cucumber, peeled and diced
¼ teaspoon turmeric	
pinch of cayenne pepper	1 teaspoon salt
pinch of black pepper	½ cup water
1 teaspoon green pepper, finely chopped	2 cups buttermilk
	1 teaspoon vegetable oil
½ teaspoon mustard seeds	

Heat vegetable oil and fry onion until golden. Add cumin, turmeric, cayenne pepper, black pepper, green pepper and coconut. Fry for 2 or 3 minutes. Add cucumber, salt and water. Cover and simmer until cucumber is tender. Remove from heat and cool. Combine with buttermilk.

In the remaining teaspoon of oil, fry the mustard seeds until they pop. Add to the cucumber-buttermilk mixture.

In India this preparation is served at room temperature; however, you may wish to chill it before serving.

Mulligatawny Soup

1 tablespoon ground coriander	2 cloves garlic, crushed
1 teaspoon cumin	4 onions, chopped
1 teaspoon turmeric	2 cups water or stock
1 teaspoon poppy seeds	1 tablespoon oil
1 teaspoon salt	1 cup coconut milk
1 teaspoon lemon juice	

Combine coriander, cumin, turmeric, poppy seeds, salt, garlic, half of the chopped onions and the stock. Simmer for 25 minutes and strain. Meanwhile, sauté other half of the onions in the oil until brown. Add to strained stock along with coconut milk and lemon juice. Simmer for 4 to 5 minutes.

Chicken Coconut Soup

2 fresh coconuts	1 teaspoon coriander
5 cups water	½ teaspoon cumin
3 tablespoons vegetable oil	¼ teaspoon cayenne pepper
2 medium onions, chopped	1 frying chicken, 2 to 2½
1 teaspoon grated ginger	pounds, disjointed
2 cloves garlic, crushed	2 teaspoons salt
2-inch stick of cinnamon	2 medium tomatoes, peeled and
2 whole cardamoms	chopped
1 teaspoon turmeric	accompaniments (*see below*)

Grind coconuts in a food mill or electric blender. Combine with 3 cups water and bring to a boil. Set aside for 1 hour. Strain, extracting as much liquid as possible. Set aside.

Heat vegetable oil and fry onions until golden. Add ginger, garlic, cinnamon, cardamoms, turmeric, coriander, cumin and cayenne pepper. Fry for 2 or 3 minutes. Put in chicken and cook for 5 minutes. Sprinkle in salt and add tomatoes. Pour in the remaining 2 cups water. Cover and simmer until chicken is tender. Add extracted coconut liquid and simmer, uncovered, for 10 minutes.

Serve in a tureen, surrounded with separate bowls of the following accompaniments which each person can add to his soup:

1. Hot, cooked small macaroni
2. Chopped fresh coriander leaves, or chopped parsley and chives
3. Wedges of lemon or lime
4. Chili powder
5. Fried onion rings

This is a Burmese dish which has found its way to India.

Coconut Moong Dhal

1 cup whole moong beans soaked for 1 hour	1 small onion, grated
	1 bay leaf, crumbled
boiling water	¼ teaspoon cumin
⅓ cup grated, unsweetened coconut	¼ teaspoon turmeric
	1 teaspoon salt
2 fresh or pickled green chilies, finely chopped	2 tablespoons vegetable oil
	1 small onion, thinly sliced

Drain moong beans and cover with just enough boiling water to cook them without burning. When cooked and very little moisture remains, add coconut, chopped green chilies, grated onion, bay leaf, cumin, turmeric and salt. Mix thoroughly and simmer, covered, over very low heat for 5 minutes.

Meanwhile, brown sliced onion in the vegetable oil. Remove moong beans from heat and stir in the browned onion. Serve very hot.

Moong beans are available in Chinese and Japanese markets as well as in many health food shops. You could substitute lentils, if absolutely necessary.

Spicy Chick-peas

1 cup chick-peas or canned garbanzos	3 medium tomatoes, peeled and chopped
5 cups water	¼ teaspoon cumin
2 tablespoons vegetable oil	1½ teaspoons salt
1 large onion, finely chopped	pinch of ground cinnamon
3 cloves garlic, crushed	pinch of ground cloves
1 tablespoon green pepper, minced	pinch of black pepper
½ teaspoon turmeric	2 tablespoons lemon juice
½ teaspoon cayenne pepper	fresh coriander leaves or chopped parsley and chives

Soak chick-peas 10 to 12 hours in 5 cups water. Boil in the same water until soft. Drain and reserve liquid. If canned garbanzos are used, do not soak, but reserve the liquid in can.

Heat vegetable oil and fry the onion until golden. Add

garlic, green pepper, turmeric and cayenne. Fry for 2 or 3
minutes. Put in tomatoes, cumin, salt, cinnamon, cloves and
black pepper. Cook for 5 minutes. Add the chick-peas and
¾ cup of the reserved cooking liquid. Simmer for 15 minutes.
Stir in lemon juice. Serve garnished with coriander leaves.

Indian Split Pea Soup

1 cup split green peas, soaked 1 hour	1 teaspoon turmeric
	1 teaspoon cumin
4 tablespoons vegetable oil	½ teaspoon crushed red pepper
1 large onion, chopped	2 teaspoons salt
2 pounds soup bones	2 medium tomatoes, peeled and chopped
1 clove garlic, crushed	
2-inch stick of cinnamon	5 cups boiling water
2 cloves	1 medium onion, sliced
2 whole cardamoms, bruised	1 tablespoon vegetable oil
¼ teaspoon peppercorns	chopped green onion
½ teaspoon minced ginger	fresh coriander leaves, optional

Heat vegetable oil and brown the chopped onion. Add soup
bones, garlic, cinnamon, cloves, cardamoms, peppercorns, ginger, turmeric, cumin, red pepper and salt. Fry for 5 minutes.
Add tomatoes and cook for 5 minutes. Put in drained peas.
Stir for several minutes.

Cover with boiling water and simmer for 2 or 3 hours. Just
before serving, brown the sliced onion in 1 tablespoon oil and
stir into soup.

Serve garnished with chopped green onion and fresh coriander leaves.

Amti

¾ cup yellow split peas	½ teaspoon paprika
1½ cups boiling water (about)	⅛ teaspoon crushed black
2 tablespoons vegetable oil	pepper
½ teaspoon mustard seeds	pinch of ground cinnamon
3 fresh or pickled green chilies,	pinch of ground cloves
finely chopped, or to taste	pinch of ground cardamom
1 small onion, finely chopped	1 tablespoon lemon juice
½ teaspoon turmeric	½ teaspoon brown sugar
1 teaspoon salt	

Soak split peas for 1 hour. Drain. Add boiling water and cook until soft, about 30 minutes.

Heat vegetable oil and fry mustard seeds until they pop. Put in the green chilies and onion. Fry until golden. Add turmeric, paprika, black pepper, cinnamon, cloves and cardamom. Fry for 2 minutes. Stir into the cooked split peas. Bring to a simmer and add lemon juice, brown sugar and salt. Mix well and serve.

Dhal

1 cup split yellow peas, soaked	1 small onion, chopped
1 hour	1 teaspoon turmeric
3 cups water	¼ teaspoon cayenne pepper
2 tablespoons vegetable oil	1½ teaspoons salt
1 tablespoon lemon juice	

Bring water to a boil and stir in the drained split yellow peas. Cover and let simmer.

Meanwhile, heat the vegetable oil and fry the onion until golden. Add turmeric and cayenne pepper and fry for a minute or two. Stir into the simmering peas. Cover and continue simmering until peas are soft — about 30 minutes. Add salt and lemon juice. Stir well.

If desired, a ripe mango could be sliced and added, or ⅓ cup coconut or both. This dish could be garnished with chopped coriander leaves or mint leaves, too.

Buttermilk Curry

¼ cup grated unsweetened coconut	2 tablespoons vegetable oil
	1 teaspoon mustard seeds
¼ teaspoon turmeric	1 teaspoon fenugreek seeds
¼ teaspoon cayenne pepper	1 bay leaf, crumbled
pinch of cumin	2 slices ginger
1 small onion	1 quart buttermilk
1½ teaspoons salt or to taste	

Whirl together in electric blender or grind in a food mill the coconut, turmeric, cayenne, cumin and onion.

Heat oil and fry mustard seeds and fenugreek seeds until they crackle. Add bay leaf, ginger and coconut-spice mixture. Fry for 2 or 3 minutes. Add buttermilk and bring just to the boiling point, stirring constantly. Do *not* boil. Remove from heat and stir occasionally until cool.

X. EGGS

EGG CURRIES are popular throughout India, and are an excellent source of protein. The eggs are hard-cooked and cut in half or sometimes quartered and put into a rather thick sauce. Hard-cooked eggs can be used as a substitute in any of the meat or vegetable recipes in this book as well as in those specifically given for eggs. In place of any main ingredient, add halved eggs and simmer 10 minutes.

Parsi Omelet

6 eggs, separated	2 tablespoons chopped corian-
2 tablespoons milk	der leaves, optional
½ teaspoon baking powder	1 green onion, finely chopped
½ teaspoon salt	pinch of turmeric
2 fresh or pickled green chilies,	pinch of cumin
finely chopped	2 tablespoons clarified butter

Beat egg yolks with milk and baking powder. Beat egg whites
with salt until stiff but not dry. Combine green chilies, coriander leaves (if used), green onion, turmeric and cumin with
egg yolks, and fold into beaten whites. Melt butter in skillet
and add egg mixture. Cook on top of stove about 10 minutes.
Then put in 300° oven until top is set. Cut slashes on each
side and fold in half. Serve at once.

Eggs Akuri

6 eggs	½ teaspoon salt
1 medium onion, thinly sliced	¼ cup milk
1 tablespoon chives	2 tablespoons clarified butter
3 fresh or pickled green chilies,	1 fresh or pickled green chili,
finely chopped	chopped
½ teaspoon cumin, powdered	

Sauté onion till golden in 1 tablespoon of butter. Add chives
and 3 green chilies. Beat eggs with milk and salt. Add other
tablespoon of butter to pan and when this is melted, pour in
the eggs. Scramble with fork. When done, garnish with

additional green chili, finely chopped, and sprinkle top with powdered cumin.

Khagina

3 eggs   pinch of ground cardamom
¼ cup yogurt   pinch each of salt and pepper
¼ teaspoon ground coriander   1 large onion, thinly sliced
2 tablespoons clarified butter

Beat together the eggs, yogurt, coriander, cardamom, salt and pepper. Sauté onion in butter until golden. Add egg mixture and cook over low heat as a regular omelet. Fold and serve.

Egg and Potato Curry

1 large onion, thinly sliced   ¼ teaspoon fenugreek
1 fresh or pickled green chili,   1-inch stick of cinnamon
finely chopped   ¼ bay leaf, crumbled
2 cloves garlic, crushed   ½ teaspoon salt
¼ teaspoon ginger, finely   2 medium potatoes, cooked and
chopped   quartered
2 tablespoons vegetable oil   1¼ cups coconut milk
¼ teaspoon turmeric   4 hard-cooked eggs, halved
1 tablespoon lime juice

Fry onion, green chili, garlic and ginger in oil for 5 minutes. Add turmeric, fenugreek, cinnamon, bay leaf, and stir for 2 or 3 minutes. Put in salt, potatoes, coconut milk and eggs. Sim-

mer, uncovered for 10 minutes. Remove from heat and stir
in lime juice.

Eggs with Coconut

3 tablespoons clarified butter	¼ bay leaf, finely crumbled
2 tablespoons onion, finely chopped	4 eggs
	4 tablespoons milk
½ cup grated unsweetened coconut	¼ teaspoon salt
	⅛ teaspoon chili powder

In skillet sauté onion in butter for a minute or two. Add
coconut and finely crumbled bay leaf. Beat together eggs,
milk, salt and chili powder. Pour into skillet and when eggs
begin to thicken, stir, until well scrambled.

Madras Omelet Curry

4 eggs	2 tablespoons ground coriander
4 tablespoons milk	¼ teaspoon ginger, finely chopped
½ teaspoon salt	
1 tablespoon clarified butter	½ teaspoon chili powder
2 medium potatoes, cooked and cut in half-inch slices	pinch each of turmeric and cinnamon
2 medium onions, sliced	½ bay leaf
2 tablespoons vegetable oil	1½ cups coconut milk
2 cloves	½ teaspoon salt
1 teaspoon lime juice	

Beat eggs, milk and salt together. Melt butter and make an
omelet. Fold in half and cut into ½-inch strips.

Heat oil and brown onions. Remove half of them and set aside for garnishing. To the remaining onions in pan, add cloves, coriander, ginger, chili powder, turmeric, cinnamon and bay leaf. Fry for a minute or two. Put in coconut milk and salt; simmer for 5 minutes. Add potato slices and omelet strips and continue simmering until thoroughly heated. Remove from heat. Stir in lime juice. Garnish with reserved browned onion.

Variation: Instead of omelet strips, poached eggs can be added just before serving.

Baked Eggs and Okra

1 medium onion, finely chopped	¼ teaspoon turmeric
2 tablespoons vegetable oil	1 teaspoon salt
1 pound okra, sliced	3 medium tomatoes, peeled and
½ teaspoon chili powder	chopped
½ teaspoon coriander	⅓ cup water
½ teaspoon cumin	4 eggs

Fry onion until golden in vegetable oil. Add okra, chili powder, coriander, cumin, turmeric and salt. Cook for 5 minutes, stirring frequently. Put in tomatoes and water. Simmer another 5 minutes. More water can be added if it gets too dry. Remove from heat and spread in a greased baking dish.

Make slight dents in sauce and break eggs into them. Bake at 350° for about 10 to 12 minutes.

In India, the eggs would be done in a pan with live coals put on the lid.

Egg and Split Pea Curry

½ cup split yellow peas	1 tablespoon vegetable oil
1 teaspoon salt	1 teaspoon ground coriander
1½ cups boiling water	1 teaspoon poppy seeds, crushed
½ teaspoon turmeric	pinch of cumin
¼ teaspoon crushed red pepper	1 cup coconut milk
1 small onion, finely chopped	4 hard-cooked eggs, halved
1 tablespoon lime juice	

Soak split peas in water to cover for 1 hour. Drain. Add peas to boiling water along with salt, turmeric, crushed red pepper. Cover and simmer until soft (about 30 to 40 minutes). Beat with whisk.

Meanwhile, sauté onion until golden in hot oil. Put in coriander, poppy seeds and cumin. Fry another 2 or 3 minutes. Stir this mixture into cooked split peas and add coconut milk. Simmer a minute or two. Put in eggs and heat. Add lime juice.

Spicy Tomato Eggs

2 medium onions, thinly sliced	3 medium tomatoes, peeled and chopped
2 tablespoons vegetable oil	¾ cup water
1 teaspoon chili powder or to taste	1 tablespoon lime juice
1 tablespoon ground coriander	4 hard-cooked eggs, halved
pinch of turmeric and cumin	1 tablespoon chopped coriander leaves, optional
1 teaspoon grated ginger	
1 teaspoon salt	

Heat oil and fry the onions until golden brown. Add chili

powder, ground coriander, turmeric, cumin and ginger; fry for a minute or two. Put in salt and tomatoes. Cook for several minutes. Add water and simmer until sauce thickens slightly. Add lime juice, stirring well. Put in eggs and heat through. Garnish with chopped coriander leaves.

Egg and Vegetable Curry

1 large onion, chopped	1 large carrot, peeled and sliced
3 tablespoons vegetable oil	½ cup green beans, cut up
1 teaspoon ground coriander	1 cup shredded cabbage
½ teaspoon chili powder	1 medium potato, diced
pinch of turmeric	2 tablespoons tomato paste
1 tablespoon chopped coriander	1 teaspoon salt
leaves	1 cup boiling water
4 hard-cooked eggs, halved	

Fry onion in hot oil for 5 minutes. Add ground coriander, chili powder, turmeric and coriander leaves; continue cooking for several minutes. Put in carrot, green beans, cabbage, potato, tomato paste, salt and boiling water. Cover and simmer until vegetables are tender. Put in hard-cooked eggs and simmer about 5 minutes longer.

For coriander leaves you may substitute 1 teaspoon chives and 1 teaspoon parsley.

Egg Moilee

2 medium onions, thinly sliced	pinch of turmeric
2 tablespoons vegetable oil	1/4 cup tomato paste
1 fresh or pickled green chili, finely chopped	1 teaspoon salt
	1 cup green peas
1 teaspoon cumin	1 1/2 cups coconut milk
1 teaspoon grated ginger	4 hard-cooked eggs, halved
1 teaspoon lime juice	

Fry the onions in the oil until brown, put in green chili, cumin, ginger and turmeric; fry for another minute or two. Add tomato paste, salt, green peas and coconut milk. Simmer until peas are tender. Add eggs and heat. Sprinkle with lime juice.

Spicy Eggs

1 large onion, finely chopped	1/2 teaspoon salt
2 tablespoons vegetable oil	pinch of black pepper
1 teaspoon chili powder or to taste	1/2 cup grated unsweetened coconut
1/4 teaspoon cinnamon	1/2 cup water
1/8 teaspoon ground cloves	4 hard-cooked eggs

Brown onion in hot oil. Add chili powder, cinnamon, cloves, salt and black pepper. Fry for a minute or two. Stir in coconut and then pour in water. Simmer 5 minutes. Prick eggs all over with fork or sharp instrument. Add to sauce and bring to a boil, turning constantly. Remove from heat.

Mild Egg Curry

1 medium onion, chopped
1 tablespoon vegetable oil
¼ teaspoon crushed black pepper
2 teaspoons cumin
½ teaspoon turmeric
1 teaspoon salt
1 cup water

2 medium potatoes, cooked and halved
4 hard-cooked eggs, halved
½ teaspoon lemon juice
2 small tomatoes, quartered
1 tablespoon chopped coriander leaves

Brown onion in hot oil. Add pepper, cumin and turmeric; fry for a minute or two. Put in salt and water; bring to a boil. Add potatoes and eggs. Simmer 10 minutes. To serve: garnish with tomato quarters and coriander leaves. Sprinkle with lemon juice.

XI. BREADS

SINCE WHEAT is second only to rice among India's staple
foods, bread made from wheat flour is one of the mainstays
of a meal in northern and western India, where the major
supply of wheat is grown. Indian bread, however, can be
made of many different grains, including rice. It can be
leavened or unleavened and cooked thick or thin, depending
on individual preference and the quality of the cook.

The most popular of the North Indian breads are chappatis, eaten by millions every day. When they are made thin and puffed up, they are known as *phulka* and remind one of a flour tortilla. Phulka are usually found in the homes of middle to upper class families.

Other breads popular throughout India: Parathas are very rich, flaky fried breads. The dough is repeatedly brushed with butter, folded and rerolled. *Pooris* are similar to chappatis and parathas except that they are a little smaller and are fried in deep fat. *Nan*, which is baked on the inside walls of a 4- or 5-foot clay oven called a *tandoor*, is a particularly popular accompaniment to *tandoori* chicken, usually cooked on a large skewer in the same oven.

In the South, wheat flour is not used so extensively, since more rice is grown and consumed in that area with the emphasis on bread considerably diminishing.

Chappatis

2 cups whole wheat flour 1 teaspoon salt
2 cups white flour 3 tablespoons melted butter
water

Sift together the two flours and salt. Thoroughly mix in the melted butter. Add enough water to make a soft dough. Knead it well. The more you knead, the lighter it will be. Cover with a damp cloth and set aside for 1 hour.

Knead thoroughly again. Form into 8 to 10 small balls and roll out into paper-thin pieces the size of a pancake.

Heat a heavy skillet or griddle. Wipe with a greased paper towel or cloth and cook the chappatis, turning now and again until slightly browned but not hardened (about 5 to 7 minutes for each one). Wipe the griddle again after each chappati is cooked.

To serve, brush with butter and eat while very hot.

For puffiness, put cooked chappatis on lowest rack of a 350° oven for a few minutes, watching carefully.

Graham, barley, oatmeal or rice flour can be substituted for whole wheat.

Parathas

3 cups whole wheat flour	5 tablespoons clarified butter
1 cup white flour	water
1½ teaspoons salt	½ cup melted clarified butter

Sift together the flours and salt. Cut in the 5 tablespoons of butter. Add enough water to make a soft dough. Knead well. Cover with a damp cloth and set aside for at least 1 hour. Knead well again. Divide the dough into two parts. Roll out each of these parts into a rectangle about ½-inch thick. Brush with melted butter and roll up evenly in a jelly-roll fashion. Cut each of these rolls into five equal parts. Place cut side of each one up. Flatten out each paratha and roll out very thin to the size of a pancake.

Heat a heavy griddle or skillet and brush with clarified butter. Fry each paratha on both sides until crisp and brown, adding more butter around edges, if necessary. Parathas should be flaky.

For crisper parathas, substitute from 2 tablespoons to ¼ cup milk for the same amount of water when mixing the dough.

Stuffed Paratha

Paratha dough	1 clove garlic, crushed
2 tablespoons clarified butter	¼ teaspoon cayenne pepper
1 small onion, minced	1 cup mashed potatoes
¼ teaspoon finely chopped ginger	½ teaspoon salt
	Melted clarified butter

Heat 2 tablespoons butter and brown onion. Add ginger, garlic and cayenne. Fry for 2 or 3 minutes. Remove from heat and mix with mashed potatoes. Add salt.

Roll out parathas into pancakes. Spread some filling on one paratha and cover with another, sealing edges with a little milk.

Grease a griddle. Brush parathas with melted butter. Fry on both sides until crisp and brown.

One-half pound cooked ground beef or lamb may be substituted for mashed potatoes.

Stuffing Variations:

Green Peas

1 cup cooked green peas	½ teaspoon salt
1 teaspoon chopped mint leaves	¼ teaspoon cayenne pepper
pinch of turmeric	a squeeze of lime juice
¼ teaspoon cumin	1 tablespoon clarified butter

Combine all ingredients and sauté in butter for 2 or 3 minutes.

Radish (Mooli)

1 cup grated radishes	½ teaspoon chili powder
1 teaspoon grated ginger	1 teaspoon salt
1 tablespoon clarified butter	

Squeeze out excess moisture. Mix together radishes, ginger, chili powder and salt. Heat butter and cook radish mixture over low heat for 2 or 3 minutes.

Nan

1 package yeast	¼ cup yogurt
¼ cup warm water	1 cup lukewarm water
1 tablespoon sugar	1 egg, beaten
2 teaspoons salt	2¾ to 3¼ cups white flour
¼ cup melted butter	melted butter
	poppy seeds

Dissolve yeast in warm water (about 110°). Combine sugar, salt, ¼ cup melted butter, yogurt and lukewarm water. Add egg and dissolved yeast. Stir in enough flour to make a soft dough. Cover and set aside for 1 hour.

Knead on a floured board. Divide into even-sized balls. Let rest for 10 minutes.

Meanwhile, remove racks from oven and heat to 450°. Take one or two balls at a time and pat into oval or oblong pieces about ¼-inch thick. Brush tops with melted butter and sprinkle with a few poppy seeds. Carefully slip the nan onto the oven floor. Bake about 10 minutes or until the tops are puffy and brown. If they do not brown on the top as well as expected, slide them under the broiler for a minute or two. Serve very hot. Especially good with tandoori chicken.

In India, *kalonji* or *nigella*, black seeds like onion seeds, are sprinkled on the top.

Pooris

3 cups white flour   3 tablespoons melted butter
1 cup whole wheat flour   water
1 teaspoon salt   yogurt, optional
vegetable oil for deep frying

Sift together the flours and salt. Add melted butter and rub into the flour by hand. Gradually add enough water to make a stiff dough. Cover with a damp cloth and set aside for at least ½ hour.

Roll the dough very thin. Cut into 3-inch to 4-inch circles.

Heat the vegetable oil to 360° to 365°. Quickly fry the pooris, pressing down gently into the oil with a perforated spoon or pancake turner to make them puffy. When golden brown on both sides and puffed, remove from fat and drain on paper towels. Serve very hot.

Yogurt may be used instead of some of the water for more crispness.

Spicy Potato Pooris

1 pound potatoes, peeled,   1 teaspoon salt
cooked and mashed   1 teaspoon cumin
1 small onion, minced   ¼ teaspoon ground cardamom
2 tablespoons butter   ¼ teaspoon ground cloves
1½ cups white flour   ¼ teaspoon black pepper
½ cup whole wheat flour   water

Combine mashed potatoes, onion and butter. Sift together the flours, salt, cumin, cardamom, cloves and black pepper.

Combine potatoes and flour, adding water to make a pliable

dough. Set aside, covered with a damp cloth, for 30 minutes. Roll out to ¼-inch thickness. Cut in 3-inch circles and fry as in preceding recipe.

Banana Pooris

1¾ cups white flour	2 tablespoons melted butter
¼ cup whole wheat flour	¼ cup mashed bananas
1 teaspoon sugar	water
1 teaspoon salt	vegetable oil for deep frying

Sift together the flours, sugar and salt. Add melted butter and mashed bananas. Rub the mixture well. Add enough water to make a stiff but pliable dough. Cover with a damp cloth and let rest for ½ hour.

Roll out into a very thin layer. Cut in 3-inch circles and fry as regular pooris.

Serve hot, sprinkled with sugar.

Luchi

3 cups white flour	3 tablespoons butter
1 teaspoon salt	warm water
vegetable oil for deep frying	

Sift flour and salt. Rub in the butter. Add enough warm water to form a stiff dough. Knead until the dough becomes soft and smooth. Divide evenly into 12 balls. Roll each into a round about ⅛-inch thick.

Heat vegetable oil to 365° to 370°. Fry quickly on each side.

This is the Bengali equivalent of poori.

Bhakhri

2 cups white flour	¼ teaspoon turmeric
2 cups whole wheat flour	4 tablespoons butter
1 teaspoon salt	½ cup yogurt
pinch of asafetida, optional	cold water
½ teaspoon chili powder	melted, clarified butter

Sift together the flours, salt, asafetida, chili powder and turmeric. Rub in the butter. Add yogurt and form into a dough, adding as much cold water as necessary. Knead and set aside for 1 hour, covered by a damp cloth.

Knead again. Divide dough equally into even-sized balls. Roll into rounds about 4 inches in diameter.

Fry like parathas on a griddle.

Bhaturas

2 packages yeast	1 teaspoon salt
½ cup warm water	4½ cups white flour
½ cup yogurt	warm water
vegetable oil for deep frying	

Combine yeast and ½ cup warm water (110°). Set aside for

10 minutes. Mix with yogurt and salt. Add flour and enough warm water to make a fairly moist dough.

Cover and set aside for 1 hour.

Flour pastry board and roll out to ⅛-inch thickness. Cut in 3-inch circles. Fry in deep fat.

Remove from fat, drain and serve with chutney.

Appams
(Hoppers)

1 package dry yeast	1½ cups white flour
¼ cup warm water	1½ cups rice flour
1 tablespoon sugar	1 teaspoon salt
2 teaspoons melted butter	Melted clarified butter or vege-
pinch of nutmeg	table oil for frying
2 cups thin coconut milk	

Dissolve dry yeast in warm water (110°). Mix in sugar, butter and nutmeg. Stir in coconut milk. Add rice flour and white flour, adding some water, if necessary, to make a batter of thin pancake batter consistency.

Cover and let stand 1 to 2 hours. Add salt and gently stir, taking care not to over-manipulate the batter.

Place heavy skillet over heat. Grease with melted butter and put in 2 or 3 tablespoons of the batter. Quickly tilt pan to all directions to let the batter run thinly over bottom. Cover pan and cook hopper until done — this means brown around the thin edges and white pitted in the middle.

This is typically Madrasi, that is, a specialty of Madras. It is usually served with a pitcher of thick coconut milk.

Poppadums

Poppadums, eaten throughout India, are seldom made in the home, since their making is a special art as well as time-consuming. They can be paper thin like those typical of Madras or thicker like those of Bombay and the North. They are usually flavored with chili powder, asafetida and black pepper. *Poppas* are delicious with rice dishes and can be either toasted or fried quickly in hot fat until crispy.

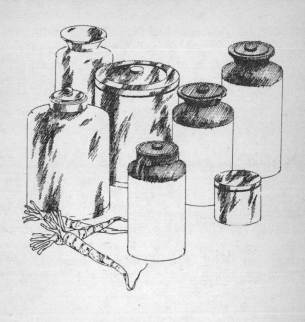

XII. PICKLES,
CHUTNEYS AND RELISHES

RICH, INDEED, is the world of Indian relishes, with countless chutneys, raitas, pickles, salads, pachadis, all of which stimulate the appetite. An Indian meal is not complete without at least one of these "tongue-tempters," and more frequently several of them in varying degree of piquancy.

In general, chutneys are made daily from vegetables, fruits or the leaves of herbs such as coriander or mint. They are usually finely chopped or ground to a paste. This is not to say, however, that all chutneys are short-keeping. It depends on the ingredients, preparation and the preference of the family.

Indian pickles are most frequently made from vegetables and fruit, although they can be made from fish or meat. They mature slowly and keep for a considerable length of time. Some of the most popular pickles made in India are mango, ginger, *kerala*, lemon and lime pickles, many of which are now exported and available in import shops throughout the United States.

Pachadis are the South Indian counterpart of the North Indian *raitas*, consisting of a most pleasing combination of yogurt seasoned with diced vegetables. Some of the pachadis are salt; while others can be sweetened.

The infinite varieties and combinations of these zesty preparations certainly bring out the best in food. Try them with a western meal, as well as an Indian one. You will be delightfully surprised and pleased.

Cucumber Pickle Parsi Style

1 pound cucumbers, sliced
6 fresh or pickled green chilies
1½-inch piece of fresh ginger, chopped
5 cloves garlic
1 cup water
3 tablespoons salt
½ cup vinegar

Mix all ingredients together. Bring to a boil. Cool and refrigerate.

Pickled Eggs

12 hard-cooked eggs	3 cups vinegar
2 teaspoons dried powdered ginger	1 teaspoon sliced fresh ginger
2 tablespoons salt	3 teaspoons mustard seeds
6 fresh or pickled green chilies, slit	3 teaspoons crushed black pepper

Mix together all ingredients except eggs and simmer for 15 minutes. Cool slightly. Prick eggs all over and place in a glass dish or jar. Pour spiced vinegar mixture over them. Refrigerate until ready for use. Will keep for some time, in refrigerator.

Lime Pickle

6 limes, washed and dried	½ teaspoon turmeric
2 tablespoons salt	2 teaspoons grated ginger
1 teaspoon crushed aniseed	1 clove garlic, crushed
1 teaspoon crushed mustard seed	1¼ cups vegetable oil (preferably mustard oil)
2 teaspoons crushed red pepper	

Cut limes in ¼-inch slices, crosswise, and combine with salt.

Heat ¼ cup of the oil (if available, use mustard oil; do *not* use olive oil) and add aniseed, mustard seed, red pepper, turmeric, grated ginger and garlic. Let simmer for 2 or 3 minutes. Remove from heat and combine with remaining oil. Add to lime slices, mixing well. Put in a jar or glass bowl, cover, and let stand at room temperature about 5 to 7 days before using. Stir occasionally. The pickles can be kept indefinitely in the refrigerator.

Cauliflower Pickle

1 medium head cauliflower	1 teaspoon crushed mustard
boiling water	seeds
1 cup vegetable oil	1 teaspoon crushed red pepper
2 teaspoons grated ginger	¼ teaspoon turmeric
1 clove garlic, crushed	2 tablespoons cider vinegar
1 teaspoon ground coriander	1 tablespoon brown sugar
1 tablespoon salt	

Wash cauliflower and break into even-sized flowerets. Bring to a boil, drain and cool. Put into a jar or glass bowl. Combine remaining ingredients, pour over cauliflower and mix thoroughly. Cover and let stand at room temperature for 4 or 5 days.

Sweet Lemon Pickle

6 lemons	pinch of cumin
2 tablespoons salt	½ cup brown sugar
½ teaspoon turmeric	½ cup vegetable oil, heated and
1 teaspoon cayenne pepper	cooled

Cut lemon in eighths and combine with salt, turmeric, cayenne pepper, cumin and brown sugar in jar or glass bowl. Pour in the oil. Mix and cover tightly. Keep in a warm place for several days, stirring occasionally. It is ready when the lemon skins are tender.

Mango Pickle I

6 ripe mangoes
2 whole green chilies
1 tablespoon salt
1 cup white vinegar
1 cup vegetable oil
2 tablespoons green chilies, finely chopped
2 tablespoons grated ginger
1 tablespoon crushed garlic

1 ½ teaspoons ground coriander
1 ½ teaspoons fenugreek seeds, crushed
1 ½ teaspoons cumin
1 ½ teaspoons whole mustard seeds
1 tablespoon ground dry mustard

Peel mangoes and cut into long slices. Add whole green chilies, salt and vinegar.

Heat vegetable oil and fry chopped green chilies, grated ginger and crushed garlic for 2 or 3 minutes. Remove from heat and add ground coriander, fenugreek seeds, cumin and whole mustard seeds. Pour over mangoes. When cool, mix ground mustard with enough water to form a paste. Mix thoroughly with mangoes. Bottle tightly.

Mango Pickle II

6 ripe mangoes	1 tablespoon mustard seeds
3 tablespoons salt	1 tablespoon cayenne pepper
2 tablespoons chopped garlic	1 tablespoon ground dry mustard
6 whole green chilies	tard
2 cups white vinegar	1 cup vegetable oil
1 tablespoon ground coriander	3 bay leaves

Peel and slice mangoes. Combine them with 2 tablespoons salt and set aside to marinate overnight.

Combine chopped garlic and whole green chilies with remaining tablespoon of salt and set aside overnight.

The next day drain off excess moisture from mangoes and pat dry.

Combine vinegar, coriander, mustard seeds, cayenne pepper and ground dry mustard, along with chopped garlic and whole green chilies. Add vegetable oil and bay leaves. Mix thoroughly and cover tightly. Stir daily for several days.

Mango Pickle with Peanuts

1 cup ripe mangoes, peeled and diced	2 tablespoons clarified butter
	¼ cup vegetable oil
1 cup green mangoes, peeled and diced	¼ teaspoon mustard seeds
	½ teaspoon fenugreek seeds
2 teaspoons salt	½ teaspoon whole peppercorns
½ teaspoon dry ginger (powder)	½ teaspoon ground coriander
¼ teaspoon cayenne pepper	3 cloves garlic, crushed
¼ teaspoon turmeric	¼ cup vinegar
½ cup peanuts	1 teaspoon brown sugar

Combine diced mangoes, salt, dry ginger, cayenne pepper and turmeric. Fry peanuts in clarified butter and add to mangoes.

Heat vegetable oil and fry mustard seeds, fenugreek seeds and peppercorns until they pop. Add ground coriander and crushed garlic. Fry for 2 minutes. Cool and add to mangoes, along with the vinegar and brown sugar. Mix thoroughly. Spoon into jar and cover tightly until ready to use.

Ginger Pachadi

1½-inch piece fresh ginger
3 tablespoons onion, finely chopped
1 fresh or pickled green chili, finely chopped
½ teaspoon salt
3 tablespoons grated unsweetened coconut
1 cup yogurt
¼ teaspoon mustard seeds
1 teaspoon vegetable oil

Slice ginger and soak in water for 1 hour. Drain. Barely cover sliced ginger, onion and green chili with water in a small saucepan and simmer 5 to 7 minutes. Drain. Mix coconut with yogurt, then add cooked ginger-mixture.

Fry mustard seeds in oil until they crackle. Stir into yogurt along with salt.

Banana Pachadi

2 cups sliced bananas
¼ cup grated unsweetened
     coconut
2 teaspoons sugar
1 cup yogurt

¼ teaspoon salt
juice of ½ lime
pinch of cayenne pepper
1 teaspoon clarified butter
¼ teaspoon mustard seeds

Combine banana slices, coconut, sugar, yogurt, salt, lime juice and cayenne pepper.

Heat butter and fry mustard seeds until they crackle. Stir into banana mixture.

Onion Pachadi
(Sweet Version)

3 large onions, thinly sliced
½ teaspoon salt
1 cup yogurt

⅓ cup sugar
¼ cup grated unsweetened
     coconut

Combine onions and salt. Set aside for one half hour. Squeeze out excess moisture. Add yogurt, sugar and grated coconut. Mix well.

Onion Pachadi
(Salt Version)

3 large onions, thinly sliced
1 teaspoon salt
1 cup yogurt
1 fresh or pickled green chili,
     finely chopped

½ cup grated unsweetened
     coconut
2 teaspoons finely chopped cori-
     ander leaves

Combine onions and salt. Set aside for ½ hour. Press out excess moisture and combine with yogurt, green chili, coconut and chopped coriander leaves.

If coriander leaves are not available, substitute 1 teaspoon parsley and 1 teaspoon chives.

Eggplant Pachadi

3 tablespoons vegetable oil
1 teaspoon mustard seeds
1 medium eggplant, peeled and diced
1 tablespoon green pepper, finely chopped
¼ teaspoon cayenne pepper
½ teaspoon salt
¼ cup water
1 cup yogurt
2 tablespoons coriander leaves, finely chopped

Heat oil and fry the mustard seeds until they pop. Put in the eggplant, green pepper, cayenne pepper and salt. Fry for 5 minutes, stirring frequently. Add water, cover and simmer until eggplant cooks to a pulp. Add water if it begins to stick. Remove from heat and cool.

When cold, add yogurt and chopped coriander leaves (or parsley and chives). Mix well.

Tomato Pachadi

2 cups chopped tomatoes
1 medium onion, finely chopped
1 fresh or pickled green chili, finely chopped
2 tablespoons chopped coriander leaves
2 teaspoons sugar
½ teaspoon salt
1 cup yogurt

Combine all ingredients and mix well. This is best if made several hours before serving.

Cabbage Raita

2 cups cabbage, shredded
1 cucumber, peeled and grated
2 tablespoons minced green
pepper

¼ teaspoons cayenne pepper
½ teaspoon black pepper
1 teaspoon salt
2 cups yogurt

Soak cabbage in ice water for 1 hour. Drain and dry thoroughly. Combine all ingredients and chill well before serving.

Cauliflower and Pea Raita

1 cup cauliflower flowerets, cut
in small pieces
1 cup green peas

1 cup yogurt
½ teaspoon salt
¼ teaspoon cumin
chili powder

Cook cauliflower and peas in salted water. Drain and chill. Mix with yogurt, salt and cumin. Sprinkle chili powder over top.

Potato Raita

3 medium potatoes
½ teaspoon cumin
½ teaspoon chili powder
1 teaspoon salt

3 fresh or pickled green chilies,
chopped
2 cups yogurt
1 bunch mint

Boil potatoes. When cold, peel them and cut into thin slices.

Combine yogurt, cumin, chili powder, salt, green chilies and half of the mint sprigs which have been finely chopped. Add to the potato slices and mix well. Garnish with remaining mint sprigs.

Onion Raita

2 large onions, thinly sliced	1 tablespoon chopped mint
½ teaspoon cumin	leaves
½ teaspoon salt	dash of tobasco sauce
1 cup yogurt	

Combine all ingredients and chill until ready for use. Stir well to mix before serving.

Spinach Raita

1 bunch spinach	½ teaspoon salt
1 tablespoon vegetable oil	1½ cups yogurt
1 teaspoon ground cumin	¼ teaspoon cayenne pepper,
1 teaspoon mustard seeds	optional
1 teaspoon fenugreek seeds	

Wash and chop spinach. Steam. Squeeze out any excess moisture.

Heat vegetable oil and fry the ground cumin, mustard and fenugreek seeds until they crackle. Add to yogurt along with spinach, salt and cayenne pepper. Mix thoroughly.

Onion and Yogurt Salad

3 large onions, finely sliced
1 teaspoon salt
1 large tomato, chopped
2 fresh or pickled green chilies, finely chopped
1 tablespoon chopped coriander leaves, optional
1 cup yogurt

Mix salt with onion rings and set aside for 20 minutes. Drain. Combine with rest of the ingredients, mixing well. Serve ice cold.

Parsi Cucumber Salad

2 medium cucumbers
1½ teaspoons salt
½ cup peanuts, chopped
1 tablespoon toasted sesame seeds
1 tablespoon grated unsweetened coconut
½ teaspoon chopped preserved ginger
½ teaspoon chili powder
pepper to taste
juice of 1 lemon

Peel and thinly slice cucumbers. Mix in salt and set aside for ½ hour. Squeeze out all water and chill the cucumbers well. Combine all ingredients.

Indian Cabbage Salad

4 cups cabbage, shredded
1 small onion, finely chopped
1 teaspoon fresh or pickled green chili, finely chopped
1 teaspoon salt

3 tablespoons coriander leaves, finely chopped, optional
2 tablespoons vegetable oil
juice of 2 limes

Combine all ingredients and mix well.

Mango Salad

3 large mangoes, diced
½ cup grated unsweetened coconut
1 fresh or pickled green chili, finely chopped

1 tablespoon sugar
¼ teaspoon salt
¾ cup yogurt
2 teaspoons clarified butter
¼ teaspoon mustard seeds

Combine diced mangoes, coconut, chopped green chili, sugar, salt and yogurt.

Heat butter and fry mustard seeds until they crackle. Cool a few minutes and add to mangoes. Mix well.

Carrot Salad

4 to 5 large carrots, grated
¼ cup yogurt
½ teaspoon salt
pinch of black pepper

2 teaspoons clarified butter
¼ teaspoon mustard seeds
1 small fresh or pickled green chili, finely chopped

Combine carrots, yogurt, salt and black pepper. Refrigerate.

Heat butter and fry mustard seeds until they crackle. Add chopped green chili and fry for 2 minutes. Remove from heat and cool. Add to carrots. Mix well and serve.

Papaya Cuchumber

2 small ripe papayas, finely chopped
juice of 1 lemon
½ teaspoon salt
pinch of asafetida, optional

2 green chilies, finely chopped
2 tablespoons grated unsweetened coconut
a few coriander leaves, optional

Combine papayas, salt and lemon juice. Set aside for 20 minutes. Drain. Add green chilies, coconut, coriander leaves and asafetida. Mix and serve. Cucumber can be substituted for the papaya.

Tomato Cuchumber

3 large tomatoes, peeled and diced
⅓ cup green pepper, finely chopped

3 tablespoons onion, finely chopped
juice of ½ lime
1 teaspoon salt

Combine all ingredients.

Cucumber Cuchumber

2 cucumbers, peeled and diced
1 small onion, finely chopped
1 fresh or pickled green chili,
    finely chopped

1 teaspoon salt
juice of 1 lime
1½ teaspoons chopped corian-
    der leaves, optional

Combine all ingredients and mix well.

Onion Cuchumber

3 large onions, thinly sliced
1 teaspoon fresh or pickled
green chili, finely chopped
1 teaspoon salt

1 tablespoon lime juice
1 tablespoon chopped coriander
    leaves, optional

Combine all ingredients and mix well.

Orange and Date Chutney

2 large oranges
1½ pounds dates, pitted
1 pound onions
1 clove garlic
½ pound raisins
5 cups white vinegar
1 teaspoon nutmeg

2 cups sugar
1 tablespoon salt
2 teaspoons chili powder
2 tablespoons grated fresh
    ginger
1 teaspoon cinnamon

Grate rind of 1 orange; peel the other one. Remove white
pith from both oranges. Dice them and grind along with the
ungrated orange peel, dates, onions, garlic and raisins. Mean-

while mix vinegar with grated orange rind, sugar, salt, chili powder, ginger, cinnamon and nutmeg. Bring to a boil and add ground fruit. Bring back to a boil and cook 5 minutes. Lower heat and simmer gently for 1 hour. When cold, bottle and store in a cool place.

Coconut Chutney

½ cup grated unsweetened coconut
1 tablespoon chopped mint leaves

¼ teaspoon cayenne pepper
½ teaspoon salt
pinch of cumin
juice of 1 lemon

Combine all ingredients.

Pineapple Chutney

1 large pineapple
2 tablespoons vegetable oil
¼ teaspoon mustard seed
1 small onion, finely chopped
½ teaspoon ground cardamom

2 fresh or pickled green chilies finely chopped
⅔ cup sugar
½ teaspoon salt

Core and finely dice pineapple.

Heat vegetable oil and fry mustard seeds until they pop. Add onion and green chilies and fry for 5 minutes. While it is still hot, add onion mixture to diced pineapple along with sugar. Mix thoroughly. Let stand 1 hour. Mix in salt and ground cardamom.

This is best when allowed to stand at least several hours.

Coriander Chutney

1 cup fresh coriander leaves	¼ teaspoon cumin
2 cloves garlic	1 teaspoon salt
2 fresh or pickled green chilies	1 tablespoon lemon juice
pinch of sugar	

Combine all ingredients in electric blender and grind until smooth.

Mint Chutney

1 cup fresh mint leaves	½ teaspoon salt
4 green onions	pinch of cumin
1 teaspoon sugar	¼ teaspoon cayenne pepper
2 tablespoons lemon juice	

ombine all ingredients in electric blender and grind smooth. Use only fresh mint leaves.

Date Chutney

½ pound dates	1 teaspoon salt
1 teaspoon turmeric	2 fresh or pickled green chilies
1 tablespoon coriander leaves	juice and pulp of 1 lemon
1 tablespoon water	

Remove pits from dates and grind with other ingredients.

Coconut and Coriander Leaf Chutney

½ cup grated unsweetened coconut
1 clove garlic
¼ teaspoon cumin
¼ cup coriander leaves

1 tablespoon lemon juice
3 fresh or pickled green chilies
1 small onion
1 teaspoon salt
4 slices ginger
pinch of sugar

Grind all ingredients together.

Raisin Chutney

1 cup raisins
1½-inch piece of ginger
5 cloves garlic
1½ teaspoons sugar

¼ teaspoon mustard seeds
¼ teaspoon cayenne pepper
½ teaspoon salt
2 tablespoons vinegar

Grind all ingredients together until smooth.

Peanut Chutney

1 cup roasted peanuts
2 cloves garlic
2 fresh or pickled green chilies
¼ cup chopped fresh coriander leaves

2 tablespoons mint leaves
1 teaspoon Worcestershire sauce
3 tablespoons lemon juice
1 teaspoon salt
pinch of sugar

In a food mill or electric blender, grind together all ingredients.

Half parsley, half chives, can be substituted for coriander leaves.

Coconut Chutney
for Idlis

¾ cup grated unsweetened coconut

2 fresh or pickled green chilies

1 teaspoon cumin

1 teaspoon mustard seeds

1 teaspoon ground coriander

1 teaspoon salt

juice and pulp of 1 lemon

2 teaspoons clarified butter

Combine coconut, green chilies, cumin, coriander, salt, lemon juice and pulp, and whirl together in an electric blender.

Heat butter and fry mustard seeds until they crackle. Combine with the coconut mixture. Serve with idlis or dosais.

XIII. SNACKS

YOUNG OR OLD, whatever their tastes in food, Indians love snacks. There are scores of intriguing snacks in Indian cookery which are usually made from infinite combinations of lentils, cereals, vegetables and meats.

Countless sidewalk vendors and foodstalls are busily preparing and cooking these delicacies seemingly twenty-four hours a day, the air filled with the aromas of food and the sound of the hawkers selling these snacks. Even at night, in village or city, one's attention is drawn by the glow of a candle or kerosene lamp to the countless piles of little fritters and pastries for sale in the streets and alleys throughout India.

Some of the favorite Indian snacks include *samosas*, a very pleasing small pastry filled with ground meat, vegetables or fish, and deep-fat fried. They never fail to satisfy and are excellent served as hors d'oeuvres. *Vadas* are another favorite. They are small doughnut-shaped pastries made up of seasoned lentils, farina, potatoes or tapioca, fried and served with some form of chutney.

In South India two of the all-time favorites are *masala dosais* which are feather-light, thin rice-and-lentil pancakes usually filled with a deliciously spiced potato mixture; and *idlis* which are a slightly fermented lentil-and-rice steamed muffin usually eaten with *sambhar*, a souplike preparation of lentils. Not only are these two eaten as snacks, but they are important breakfast items for a large population in the South.

Samosas

Pastry:

2 cups flour	⅓ cup yogurt
1 teaspoon salt	water
4 tablespoons clarified butter, melted	filling (*see below*)
	vegetable oil for deep frying

Sift together flour and salt. Add melted butter, yogurt and enough water to make a stiff dough. Knead until smooth and elastic.

Roll out very thin on a floured board. Cut into 3-inch circles. Place a teaspoon of filling in center of the circle, leaving edges free. Brush edges with a little water. Fold in half and tightly seal the edges.

Heat the vegetable oil to about 365° and fry the samosas, a few at a time, until golden brown. Drain and serve hot with fresh mint or coriander leaf chutney.

Meat Filling:

2 tablespoons vegetable oil	¼ teaspoon turmeric
1 small onion, finely chopped	½ pound ground lamb or beef
1 clove garlic, crushed	1 teaspoon salt
¼ teaspoon minced ginger	1 tablespoon lemon juice
¼ teaspoon cayenne pepper	1 tablespoon chopped fresh cori-
1 teaspoon cumin	ander or mint leaves
½ teaspoon ground coriander	

Heat vegetable oil and brown the onion. Add garlic, ginger, cayenne, cumin, coriander and turmeric. Fry for 2 or 3 minutes. Add ground meat and stir well to break up the lumps. Sprinkle with salt. Cook until all moisture is absorbed. Remove from heat and drain off excess fat. Sprinkle on lemon juice and add chopped coriander or mint leaves.

Vegetable Filling:

2 tablespoons vegetable oil	¼ teaspoon cayenne pepper
1 small onion, finely chopped	½ cup mashed potatoes
1 clove garlic, crushed	¼ cup cooked, diced carrots
½ teaspoon minced ginger	¼ cup cooked green peas
1 teaspoon minced fresh corian-	1 teaspoon salt
der leaves, optional	2 teaspoons lemon juice

Heat vegetable oil and sauté the onion until golden. Add the garlic, ginger, coriander leaves and cayenne. Fry for 2 or 3 minutes. Remove from heat. Mix in the mashed potatoes, carrots, peas, salt and lemon juice.

Chudva

3 tablespoons clarified butter	⅓ cup fresh coconut, thinly sliced
¼ teaspoon turmeric	
½ teaspoon cumin	2 tablespoons raisins
1 teaspoon sesame seeds	1½ cups puffed rice cereal
⅓ cup peanuts	1½ teaspoons salt
⅓ cup cashew nuts	¼ teaspoon cayenne pepper
pinch of garlic powder	

Heat clarified butter and fry turmeric and cumin for a minute or two. Add sesame seeds, peanuts, cashew nuts, sliced coconut and raisins. Fry until ingredients are golden brown. Toss well with puffed rice cereal, salt, cayenne pepper and garlic powder.

If preferred, a pinch of ground cinnamon can be used instead of the garlic powder.

Cashew Nuts Indian Style

2 cups cashew nuts	¼ to ½ teaspoon cayenne pepper
2 tablespoons clarified butter	
1 teaspoon salt	

Heat butter and sauté cashew nuts until golden. Sprinkle on cayenne and salt.

Spiced Split Peas

2 cups yellow split peas	2 teaspoons salt
water	½ teaspoon cayenne pepper or
1 tablespoon baking soda	to taste
vegetable oil for deep frying	¼ teaspoon ground coriander
¼ teaspoon cumin	

Soak split peas in plenty of water into which the baking soda has been mixed. Let soak 12 hours. Drain well and spread out on towels to dry thoroughly.

Heat about 2 inches of vegetable oil in a heavy pan and fry a handful of peas at a time until golden brown. Skim out. Drain well. Repeat until all peas are cooked.

Sprinkle with salt, chili powder, coriander and cumin while still warm. Mix well.

Assorted Pakoras (Vegetable Fritters)

Batter:

1½ cups split pea flour or chick-	¼ teaspoon cayenne pepper
pea flour	pinch of cumin
½ teaspoon baking powder	2 teaspoons salt
½ teaspoon turmeric	water
vegetable oil for deep frying	

Vegetables:

onion	squash	eggplant
potato	spinach	cauliflower
green pepper	okra	green chilies

Batter: Sift together the flour, baking powder, turmeric, cayenne pepper, cumin and salt. Add enough water to make a thick batter. Beat well.

Use any one of the vegetables or all of them. Cut them into thin slices; or in the case of the okra, leave whole or cut in half lengthwise. The potato, squash or cauliflower can be parboiled for a few minutes first, if desired.

Dip each piece in the batter to thoroughly coat and drop into the hot vegetable oil, which should be about 365° to 370° Fry until golden, drain and serve hot with fresh mint or coriander leaf chutney.

If you wish, the vegetables can be chopped fine, mixed in the batter and dropped by the spoonful into the fat.

Uppuma

2 tablespoons cashew nuts	1 teaspoon chopped coriander
5 tablespoons clarified butter	leaves, optional
½ teaspoon mustard seeds	1 teaspoon salt
1 small onion, finely chopped	¾ cup farina
¼ teaspoon crushed red pepper	4 cups boiling water
fresh lime juice, optional	

Heat 1 tablespoon of the butter and sauté cashew nuts until golden brown. Set aside.

Heat remaining 4 tablespoons of butter and fry mustard seeds until they pop. Add onion, crushed red pepper and coriander leaves. Fry until onion is golden. Add salt and farina. Stir until farina is very hot. Pour in boiling water, stir, cover, and cook over moderate heat until water is absorbed. Stir in the sautéed cashew nuts. Fresh lime juice can be sprinkled over individual servings, if desired.

Variations: Tomato Uppuma: add a large chopped tomato to the onions and fry until soft.

Cinnamon Uppuma: omit mustard seeds, and coriander leaves. Add 4 cloves and 2 sticks of cinnamon. Fry with the onions. This is a well-known breakfast and snack preparation in South India.

Rava Dosais

1¼ cups flour	¼ teaspoon cumin
½ cup farina	1 teaspoon salt
buttermilk	½ teaspoon baking soda
1 tablespoon vegetable oil	½ teaspoon baking powder
½ teaspoon mustard seeds	vegetable oil or melted clarified
1 fresh or pickled green chili, finely chopped	butter

Combine flour and farina. Add enough buttermilk to make a thick batter. Set aside in a warm place for 8 to 12 hours. (An electric heating pad is marvelous for this.) The batter should be slightly fermented for the dosais to turn out well.

Just before cooking, heat 1 tablespoon vegetable oil and fry mustard seeds until they crackle. Add green chili and cumin. Fry for a minute or two. Add to the batter, along with the salt, baking soda and baking powder. Beat well.

Heat a heavy griddle or skillet. Brush with oil or butter. Pour a large spoonful of the batter onto the griddle and spread out with the back of the spoon to form a nice round pancake. Cover with a lid. When cooked a delicate brown, turn. Do not cover after turning. If necessary pour a little oil around the edges. Serve hot with chutney or sambhar.

Rice Dosais

1½ cups raw rice	½ teaspoon baking soda
1 cup urid dhal (*see note be-low*)	1 teaspoon salt
¼ teaspoon cumin	vegetable oil or melted clarified butter
buttermilk	

Soak rice and urid dhal for 10 to 12 hours in separate dishes. Drain each and grind to a smooth paste in an electric blender. If necessary, add a little water to facilitate the grind. Combine the two pastes.

Add cumin and enough buttermilk to make a thin pouring-type batter. Beat until light. Set aside in a warm place for 12 hours to ferment.

Before cooking, add baking soda and salt. Beat well. Heat a heavy griddle or skillet. Brush with oil or butter. Pour in enough batter to form a pancake. Spread out in a very thin pancake with back of spoon. When golden brown, turn. Serve very hot with chutney or sambhar.

Variation: For *Masala Dosais,* before removing from the griddle or skillet, spread with 2 tablespoons of the following filling and fold over:

Filling:

2 tablespoons vegetable oil	¼ teaspoon turmeric
1 medium onion, finely chopped	2 large potatoes, cooked and finely diced
1 fresh or pickled green chili, finely chopped	1 teaspoon salt
½ teaspoon grated ginger	1 tablespoon lemon juice

Heat vegetable oil and fry onion and green chili until golden.

Add ginger and turmeric. Fry for a minute or two. Add potatoes and salt. Fry until heated throughout. Sprinkle on lemon juice. Fill *dosais*.

Note: Urid dhal can be found in Indian import shops. If not available, substitute ½ cup lentils for 1 cup urid dhal. In South India the proportion of urid dhal used in this preparation varies in different areas. As a general rule, the more urid used, the lighter will be the dosai.

Sooji Vadas

2 cups farina	½ teaspoon grated ginger
2 cups boiling water	1 teaspoon salt
1 small onion, minced	2 teaspoons chopped coriander
2 tablespoons chopped cashew	leaves, optional
nuts	yogurt
1 fresh or pickled green chili, finely chopped	vegetable oil for deep frying

Combine farina and boiling water in a mixing bowl. Add minced onion, cashew nuts, green chili, ginger, salt and the coriander leaves. Mix well. Add enough yogurt to make a stiff dough.

Take a ball of the dough about the size of a small egg. Pat it to a thick round about 2½ inches in diameter and make a hole in the center so that it looks like a small doughnut. Carefully slip it into the hot vegetable oil. Fry until light brown, turning occasionally. Three or four can be cooked at one time. Serve hot with chutney.

Variation: Omit onions and green chilies. Add ½ teaspoon black pepper and ½ teaspoon cumin.

Corn Vadas

1 cup chick-peas, soaked for 3 hours	2 tablespoons grated unsweetened coconut
2 cups corn kernels	1 tablespoon fresh coriander leaves, optional
½ cup cashew nuts	
1 tablespoon chopped green pepper	1 tablespoon lime juice
½-inch piece of ginger	¼ teaspoon cayenne pepper
	1 teaspoon salt
vegetable oil for deep frying	

Grind together in a food mill the soaked and drained chick-peas, corn, cashew nuts, green pepper, ginger, coconut, coriander leaves and lime juice. Mix in the cayenne pepper and salt.

Shape into small doughnuts about 2½ inches in diameter and fry in hot vegetable oil. Serve hot with chutney.

Idlis
(Steamed Rice Cakes)

1 cup raw rice 1 teaspoon salt
½ cup urid dhal or lentils ½ teaspoon baking soda

Soak rice and urid dhal or lentils in separate bowls for 4 hours. Drain and grind each one in an electric blender. Add a little water if necessary to facilitate grinding. Combine 2 pastes and beat well. Add a little water, if needed, to form a thick batter.

Set aside in a warm place (near an electric heating pad is excellent) for 12 hours. Batter must be slightly fermented.

When ready to cook, beat in the salt and baking soda. Grease muffin cups and fill them half full of batter. Place on a rack in a large kettle over boiling water. Cover and steam until done. To test, insert a toothpick. If it comes out without any batter sticking to it, the idli is cooked. Remove cups from heat and invert. Serve hot with coconut chutney or sambhar.

Note: Urid dhal, available at Indian import shops, will give a lighter product.

Variation: Masala Idli:

1 tablespoon clarified butter	1 teaspoon minced green pepper
½ teaspoon mustard seeds	2 tablespoons grated unsweet-
¼ teaspoon cayenne pepper	ened coconut
3 tablespoons minced onion	

Heat butter and fry mustard seeds until they crackle. Put in cayenne pepper, onion and green pepper. Fry until onion is transparent. Add to the idli batter just before cooking. Stir in the coconut and beat well. Cook as directed for idlis.

Nut Cutlets

3 thick slices brown bread	½ teaspoon salt
milk for soaking	dash of pepper
1 cup finely chopped cashew	1 teaspoon parsley
nuts	1 egg, beaten
¼ teaspoon chili powder	flour
¼ teaspoon cumin	vegetable oil for shallow frying

Soak bread slices in milk. Drain and squeeze out all liquid. Add nuts, chili powder, cumin, salt, pepper and parsley. Stir in egg. If unnecessarily dry, a little milk can be added. With floured hands, form mixture into patties and fry.

Bhel Poori

Pungent Chutney:

> ½ cup fresh coriander leaves   ½-inch piece ginger
> 2 fresh or pickled green chilies   1 clove garlic
> ¼ teaspoon salt

Grind together the ½ cup fresh coriander leaves, green chilies, ginger, garlic and salt. Mix in a little water if the paste is too thick. Set aside.

Sweet Chutney:

> ⅛ cup pitted dates   juice and pulp of 1 lemon
> ¼ teaspoon salt

Grind together the dates, lemon pulp and juice, and salt. Set aside.

Poori:

> 2 cups puffed rice cereal   1 small onion, chopped
> 1 cup crisp pooris, broken in   lemon juice to taste
> pieces (see page 178)   fresh coriander leaves
> 1 cup cooked potatoes, diced   crushed red pepper, optional

Combine puffed rice, *pooris*, potatoes and onion. Toss well in a large bowl, with the two chutneys. Garnish each serving with fresh coriander leaves and crushed red pepper. Serve immediately, before the crispness is lost.

This snack is especially popular in Bombay.

XIV. DESSERTS AND SWEETS

INDIANS have an unparalleled sweet tooth which in some parts of India, particularly the states of Gujarat and Maharashtra, is evidenced by the custom of beginning a meal with a sweet.

Many of the principal sweets, such a *gulab jaman*, *burfi* and *laddoos*, professionally made and sold in the bazaars, are better than those made at home. One of the reasons for this is the time-consuming process, particularly in making *khoa* which, along with a substantial amount of sugar, is the basis of a good many of the Indian sweets.

Khoa is dried fresh milk which is prepared by boiling and stirring whole milk until it dries up. When cooled, the finished product has the consistency of stiff dough. Naturally, this process takes considerable time and perseverance. In the United States, however, we can easily make *khoa* by mixing powdered milk with a little water and working it to a stiff doughlike consistency. In so doing we can recreate with ease, in our own kitchens, some of the outstanding Indian sweets.

Gulab Jaman

Gulabs:

2 cups flour	¾ teaspoon ground cardamom
2 cups dry powdered milk	½ cup butter
2 teaspoons baking powder	1 cup milk
½ teaspoon baking soda	vegetable oil for deep frying

Syrup:

3 cups sugar	4 cups water
1 tablespoon rose water	

Combine the sugar and water in a heavy saucepan and boil together to make a thick syrup. Keep warm.

Sift together the flour, powdered milk, baking powder, baking soda and ground cardamom. Cut in the butter with a pastry blender of 2 knives until mixture looks like cornmeal. Add milk and mix well. Turn out onto a lightly floured surface and knead until very smooth and elastic. Break off pieces of dough and roll into balls the size of cherries.

Heat the vegetable oil. If you are using a deep fat thermometer, the temperature should be about 335° to 340° Watch temperature carefully since these little balls will burn easily. Drop balls in, a few at a time. Fry until evenly browned. Remove and immediately drop into the warm syrup. Put gulab jamans and syrup in a serving dish and sprinkle on rose water.

These can be done a day ahead. Before serving they can be reheated in the syrup. This recipe makes about 36 gulab jamons.

This is one of the most popular sweets in India.

Cashew Nut Halva

3½ cups cashew nuts	½ cup water
2 tablespoons farina	1 cup sugar
½ cup clarified butter	2 tablespoons raisins, soaked
	pinch of salt

Grind the cashew nuts into a coarse paste.

Heat 3 tablespoons of the clarified butter and fry the farina until lightly browned. Mix with the cashew nut paste.

Combine water and sugar. Boil together to make a thin, moderately sticky syrup. Slowly add the nut-farina paste to the hot syrup, stirring constantly. Gradually add the remaining butter, mixing thoroughly. Add raisins and salt. Serve hot.

Banana Halva

4 or 5 firm, ripe bananas	½ teaspoon rose water
3 tablespoons clarified butter	½ teaspoon ground cardamom
1¼ cups water	2 tablespoons blanched sliced
⅝ cup sugar	almonds

Peel and cut banana into 1-inch pieces. Heat butter in a heavy skillet, preferably Teflon-coated. Add bananas and fry for about 5 minutes over moderate heat, stirring frequently. Remove from heat and thoroughly mash the bananas. Add ¼ cup water and return to heat. Simmer gently for 2 or 3 minutes, stirring constantly.

Combine sugar and remaining 1 cup of water. Add to bananas. Simmer gently for 15 to 20 minutes or until quite thick. Stir frequently and watch for sticking. Remove from heat and stir in rose water. If any excess butter is present, drain it off. Pour into serving dish. Garnish with ground cardamom and blanched almonds. Can be served either warm or slightly chilled.

Vanilla can be substituted for rose water.

Egg Halva
Anda Halva

1 cup evaporated milk	2 tablespoons raisins, soaked in
½ cup sugar	water
½ cup clarified butter	¾ teaspoon ground cardamom
4 eggs, beaten	(or nutmeg)
2 tablespoons chopped pistachio nuts or almonds	

Combine evaporated milk and sugar in a saucepan. Heat until the sugar is dissolved. Set aside to cool.

Melt butter in a heavy skillet and remove from heat. Add beaten eggs, stirring well. Return to heat and add sweetened milk. Add raisins and mix thoroughly. Stir constantly and briskly over low heat until mixture leaves the sides of the pan and the butter begins to separate. The mixture will be a golden color. Add ground cardamom and stir well. Pour into a shallow serving dish. Garnish with chopped nuts. Serve either hot or cooled.

Coconut may be substituted for pistachio nuts or used as an additional garnish.

Carrot Halva

1 pound carrots	¾ cup brown sugar
2½ cups milk	2 tablespoons raisins
½ cup clarified butter	1 teaspoon ground cardamom
2 tablespoons slivered almonds	

Grate carrots in electric blender.

Bring milk to a boil in a heavy pan, preferably Teflon-coated. Add grated carrots and cook until the milk has been absorbed, and the mixture is fairly thick. Stir frequently with a large spoon to prevent sticking or burning. This process will take about 1 to 1½ hours.

When mixture is thick, add butter. Cook for 20 minutes. Then put in the sugar and raisins. Stir well and continue cooking for about 15 minutes. Watch carefully! Stir in the ground cardamom.

Spread into a buttered shallow dish and decorate with slivered almonds. Can be served hot or cold.

Burfi

1 cup sugar	3 cups powdered dry milk
1½ cups water	2 teaspoons rose water
2 tablespoons melted clarified butter	¼ cup chopped pistachio nuts
	¼ teaspoon ground cardamom

Dissolve sugar in the water and cook until a thick syrup forms. Remove from heat. Add melted clarified butter. Gradually add the powdered milk, stirring constantly. Return to very low heat and stir for a minute or two. Add rose water. This should be a very thick batter. Pour into a buttered pie dish or other shallow utensil. Combine the nuts and ground cardamom. Press into the top of the mixture. When cool, cut into small squares or diamond shapes with a sharp knife. Can be decorated with thin silver leaf, if available.

Kulfi

1 tin sweetened condensed milk	½ teaspoon vanilla
1 cup heavy cream	¼ cup finely chopped almonds
¼ cup chopped pistachio nuts	

Mix together all ingredients. Pour into an ice cube tray and freeze. Serve cut in slices. This preparation has a faster melting rate than ice cream since it does not contain any gelatin. So, serve immediately.

In India kulfi is frozen in cone-shaped individual molds which are about 4 to 5 inches long and slightly flattened at the narrow end.

Rasgullas

1 quart milk, at room temperature (see note)	1 tablespoon regular farina
5 Junket rennet tablets	8–10 blanched almonds
2 tablespoons water	2 cups sugar
	2 cups water
1 tablespoon rose water	

Crush rennet tablets and dissolve in 2 tablespoons water. Stir into the milk and set aside for 1 hour. Line a sieve with a tea towel and put in the "set" milk. Allow most of the liquid to drip out; then squeeze well to remove as much excess moisture as possible. Combine with the farina, mixing and kneading thoroughly. Form into about eight or ten 1-inch balls. Press an almond into the center. *Note:* You will have to work each ball firmly into shape.

Combine the sugar and water and boil for several minutes to make a very thin syrup. Remove from heat and gently put in balls. Return to heat and simmer for about 15 to 20 minutes until balls are puffy. Be careful not to break the balls. Remove with a slotted spoon. Sprinkle with rose water or put in thick cream. Can be eaten hot or cold.

Note: 1 cup dry pot cheese can be substituted for milk. In this case, simply mix with the farina after being certain that as much moisture as possible has been removed.

Shahi Tukra

4 slices bread, cut 1-inch thick	1 cup evaporated milk
⅓ cup clarified butter	1 tablespoon chopped cashew
¼ teaspoon saffron	nuts
1 tablespoon warm water	1 tablespoon chopped pistachio
½ cup sugar	nuts
¼ cup water	¼ teaspoon ground cardamom

Bread that is several days old is best for this dish. Trim crusts off bread. Sauté bread slices in the clarified butter until golden brown, adding butter to the pan as needed. Arrange bread in a flat, heatproof serving dish without placing one slice on top of another. Set aside.

Dissolve saffron in warm water and set aside. Combine sugar and water and boil to make a thick syrup. Add milk and saffron. Stir thoroughly and heat to the boiling point. Pour over the bread slices. Garnish with chopped nuts and ground cardamom.

Can be served either warm or cold.

Phirni

2 cups milk	1 tablespoon pistachio nuts
2 tablespoons rice flour	1 tablespoon slivered, blanched
¼ cup sugar	almonds
1 teaspoon rose water	

Heat milk to boiling point in a heavy saucepan. Add rice flour and cook over low heat, stirring frequently until it becomes fairly thick. Watch carefully to see that it does not burn.

Remove from heat. Pour into flat serving dishes. Decorate with nuts and sprinkle with rose water. Cool and serve.

Jallebis

1 package dry or compressed yeast	¼ teaspoon saffron (or yellow coloring)
¼ cup warm water	3 cups sugar
3 cups flour	2 cups water
water	funnel with small spout
vegetable oil for deep frying (see note)	

Dissolve yeast in ¼ cup warm water. Combine flour, dissolved yeast and enough water to make a smooth pancake consistency batter. Add saffron and beat for several minutes. Set aside for 30 minutes.

Meanwhile, combine sugar and water; boil to make a syrup about the consistency of corn syrup. Keep warm while waiting for use.

Heat the vegetable oil in a heavy pan to about 365°. Put some of the batter in the funnel (keep your finger over the tip). Using finger to control the amount of batter, move the funnel in concentric circles over the hot fat. Cook on each side until golden and crisp. Remove and drain.

Dip each jallebi in the warm syrup for a minute or two. Drain again. Plan to eat them soon after they are made since they will not keep the proper crispness too long.

Note: If desired, half vegetable oil and half clarified butter may be used for deep frying for a richer flavor.

In India, a coconut shell with one hole is used instead of the funnel.

Shakarpara

2 cups flour	¼ teaspoon ground cardamom
pinch of salt	1 tablespoon yogurt
2 tablespoons clarified butter	water
½ cup powdered sugar	vegetable oil for frying

Sift flour and salt. Thoroughly blend in the butter. Add the powdered sugar, ground cardamom, yogurt and enough water to make a moderately stiff dough. Roll out to ¼-inch thickness. Cut into small diamonds and fry in deep fat until light brown.

Nut and Sesame Ladoo

1 cup toasted sesame seeds	½ cup brown sugar, firmly
¾ cup peanuts	packed
1 cup cashew nuts	½ cup white sugar
2 tablespoons clarified butter	½ cup water
pinch of salt	

Grind toasted sesame seeds to a paste in an electric blender.

Fry peanuts and cashew nuts to a golden brown in the clarified butter. Cool and chop finely. Combine with the ground sesame seeds.

Combine sugars and water. Bring to a boil and cook until it reaches the soft ball stage, 234° on a candy thermometer.

Stir the nut-sesame mixture into the syrup. Add salt and mix thoroughly. Grease hands and shape into balls the size of walnuts.

If the mixture is too soft to hold its shape in balls, place over low heat till firm enough to hold.

Semolina Ladoo

1⅓ cups farina   1 teaspoon ground cardamom
½ cup clarified butter   1 cup sugar
⅓ cup grated, unsweetened ½ cup water
        coconut

Dissolve sugar in water in a heavy saucepan and boil until a thick syrup forms.

Melt butter and add farina. Cook over moderate heat, stirring constantly until nicely browned. Remove from heat and add coconut and cardamom. Add syrup. When cool enough to handle, shape into even-sized small balls.

Sewian

½ pound vermicelli, broken   2 tablespoons raisins
        into 1-inch pieces   2 tablespoons chopped pistachio
5 tablespoons clarified butter   nuts
    pinch of ground cloves   pinch of saffron
    1½ cups hot milk   ½ teaspoon ground cardamom
        ¾ cup sugar   cream

Heat the butter in a heavy-bottomed saucepan. Add vermicelli and cloves. Fry until lightly browned. Add hot milk and sugar. Cover and gently simmer, stirring frequently. When half done, add the raisins, nuts, saffron and cardamom. Continue cooking until nearly dry. Serve either hot or cold with cream.

This is a very popular dish with the Muslims of India. It is frequently garnished with silver leaf.

Doodh Pak

½ cup rice	1 tablespoon slivered almonds
2½ cups milk	1 tablespoon pistachio nuts,
1 cup sugar	chopped
2 tablespoons peanuts, chopped	¼ teaspoon ground cardamom

Heat milk in a heavy saucepan. When it boils, stir in the rice. Simmer for ½ hour, stirring frequently. Add sugar and nuts. Continue cooking until mixture has thickened. Serve hot or cold sprinkled with cardamom. This is occasionally served with pooris (see Breads, Chapter XVII).

Coconut Squares

1 cup cream	2 tablespoons finely chopped
2 cups sugar	almonds
1 tablespoon butter	1 teaspoon vanilla
¾ cup grated coconut	few drops red food coloring

Combine cream, sugar and butter in a heavy saucepan and cook to the soft ball stage, 238° on a candy thermometer. Remove from heat and cool slightly. Add coconut and beat until creamy. Add almonds, vanilla and enough food coloring to make pale pink. Beat again and pour into a greased pan. Cut into small squares.

Malpuras
(Indian Sweet Pancakes)

½ cup whole wheat flour	1 cup milk
¾ cup white flour	2 tablespoons melted butter
¼ cup sugar	water
¾ teaspoon ground cardamom	melted clarified butter for
1 teaspoon baking powder	frying
pinch of salt	light corn syrup

Sift together the whole wheat flour, white flour, sugar, ground cardamom, baking powder and salt. Gradually add milk and melted butter. Beat well. If too thick, slowly add enough water to make a light-pancake type of batter. Beat thoroughly.

Heat griddle and brush with melted clarified butter. Spoon some of the batter onto the griddle. Spread it to a round of 4 inches. Pour a little of the butter around edge. When golden, turn and fry on other side. When they are done, the edges will be crispy and the center like a regular pancake. Serve hot with syrup.

Falooda

4 tablespoons sweetened condensed milk
8 tablespoons milk
4 teaspoons sugar

rose water (or raspberry syrup)
¼ cup cooked tapioca
cold water
vanilla ice cream

Use four 6-ounce glasses. Into each one, put 1 tablespoon condensed milk, 2 tablespoons milk and 1 teaspoon sugar. Sprinkle in some rose water. Add 1 tablespoon cooked tapioca. Fill three-quarters full of water. Mix well. Top with a small scoop of vanilla ice cream.

Ice cubes can be substituted for ice cream.

Zarda

¼ cup clarified butter
½ teaspoon ground cardamom
½ teaspoon ground cinnamon
1½ cups rice
1¾ cups water
1 cup milk
pinch of salt

½ cup sugar
2 tablespoons whipping cream
¼ teaspoon saffron dissolved in
1 tablespoon warm milk
2 tablespoons cashew nuts
1 tablespoon pistachio nuts
2 teaspoons clarified butter

Heat ¼ cup butter and fry cardamom and cinnamon for a minute or two. Add rice and fry for 2 or 3 minutes.

Bring water to a boil. Add rice, stir and cover tightly. When rice is half done, add milk, salt and sugar. Cover and continue cooking. When rice is done, mix in the whipping cream and saffron dissolved in the milk.

Sauté the nuts in 2 teaspoons clarified butter and garnish rice.

Shrikand

¼ teaspoon saffron
2 teaspoons warm milk
2 cups yogurt
1 cup powdered sugar
¾ teaspoon ground cardamom

1 teaspoon chopped pistachio
   nuts
2 teaspoons slivered, blanched
   almonds

Soak saffron in the warm milk. Combine yogurt, powdered sugar, soaked saffron and ground cardamom. Mix thoroughly. Garnish with pistachio nuts and almonds.

Vermicelli Payasam

¾ cup vermicelli, broken in
   1-inch pieces
3 tablespoons clarified butter
1 cup boiling water
2 cups milk

½ cup sugar
pinch of saffron
2 tablespoons raisins
2 tablespoons cashew nuts
¼ teaspoon ground cardamom

Heat 2 tablespoons of the butter and fry the vermicelli until lightly browned. Pour in the water, stir well and simmer over very low heat until the vermicelli is tender. Add the milk, sugar and saffron. Stir frequently, since the vermicelli has a tendency to stick to the bottom of the pan. Cook for 5 minutes. Meanwhile, fry raisins and cashews until lightly browned in remaining tablespoon of butter.

Remove vermicelli from heat and add raisins, cashew nuts and cardamom. Serve hot.

Coconut Candy

1½ cups brown sugar	½ cup boiling water
½ cup white sugar	4 tablespoons butter
2 tablespoons corn syrup	1½ cups shredded coconut
⅛ teaspoon salt	½ teaspoon ground cardamom

Dissolve sugars, corn syrup and salt in boiling water. Cook to the soft ball stage (about 238° on a candy thermometer). Remove from heat and stir in butter. Add coconut. Beat until it begins to harden. Add ground cardamom and pour into a greased pan. Cut into pieces when cold.

Caujas

1 cup flour	water
pinch of salt	1 cup sugar
1 tablespoon vegetable shorten-	½ cup water
ing	½ teaspoon ground cardamom
vegetable oil for deep frying	

Sift flour and salt. Thoroughly blend in the vegetable shortening. Add enough water to make a stiff dough.

Divide into 12 even-sized balls. Roll out into thin rounds. Make slits in the center. Be careful not to cut through the rounds. Holding the ends, twist each one.

Combine sugar and water; stir until sugar is dissolved, then boil to make a medium syrup.

Heat vegetable oil and fry twists until golden brown. Remove and drain. Dip in the prepared sugar syrup. Remove and sprinkle with ground cardamom. Makes 12. Instead of dipping in syrup, they can be dusted with powdered sugar.

XV. EPILOGUE

THE SCOPE of Indian cooking is enormous and inexhaustible; in fact, it is almost as vast as the subcontinent of India itself, which is the seventh largest country in the world geographically and the second most populous, with about 540 million people.

India is a land of dramatic contrasts: with one of the longest and highest mountain ranges in the world, the Himalayas, stretching from Kashmir to Burma; extremes in annual rainfall ranging from 450 inches in Cherrapungi, Assam, to about 3 inches in Saurashtra in western India; and climatic variations ranging from snow and intense cold in northern areas in winter to temperatures of 120° to 135° F. in some areas in summer. Along with its vast population, India has 14 major languages, including English, and 250 regional dialects — so one can see that these extremes and variations certainly would tend to influence the cuisine of such a vast subcontinent, along with, of course, the various religious communities. The population is about 85 percent Hindu, 10 percent Muslim, 2 percent Christian, and 3 percent Sikh, Parsi, Buddhist and Jain, combined.

In this book it has been very difficult to do much more than barely skim the surface of Indian cooking. Each recipe and method varies a bit according to the individual cook and the affluence of the family, as well as the many regional and religious influences. This book in no way claims to be a complete and comprehensive encyclopedia of Indian food preparation. It is, however, *A Taste of India* for those interested in learning more about the pleasures of Indian cuisine.

GLOSSARY

GLOSSARY

Achar – pickle.

Adrak – green ginger.

Akhni – stock.

Aloo – potato.

Ambo – ripe mango.

Arbi – yam.

Atta – whole wheat flour.

Badam – almond.

Bajri – millet.

Batakh – duck.

Bellen – rolling pin.

Besan – gram or lentil flour.

Bhārat – India.

Bhajee – a vegetable preparation, essentially dry.

Bhath – a rice dish.

Bhatura – fried bread, popular for breakfast.

Bhendi – okra.

Bhujjia – a vegetable preparation, essentially dry.

Bhurta – a vegetable preparation made by roasting vegetable in an open charcoal fire or in hot ashes and mashing it.

Biryani – a rice dish consisting of layers of partially cooked rice and curried meat cooked together until done, using a fire beneath and hot charcoal on the lid; a Moglai dish.

Brinjal – eggplant.

Bund gobi – cabbage.

Burfi – a milk sweet; rather like fudge which can be flavored with coconut, pistachios, carrots, almonds, etc.

Burra nimbu – lemon.

Chappati – also known as phulka. A thin round bread made of whole wheat and baked on a griddle. Similar to a tortilla.

Chawal – rice.

Cheeni – sugar of any kind.

Chiroti – small cakes cooked in deep fat and eaten as snacks.

Chudva – a popular mixture of different kinds of nuts, fried puffed rice, lentils, spices and sometimes raisins and coconut. Eaten as a snack.

Dahi – curds or yogurt.

Dhal – any of over 50 varieties of lentils and pulses. Also dal.

Darchini – cinnamon.

Degchis – saucepans.

Degi mirch – cayenne pepper.

Dhannia – coriander.

Dhan sak – Parsi dish containing meat and innumerable vegetables; popular in Bombay.

Doodh – milk.

Doodh pak – a milk sweet made of rice and nuts.

Do Pyaz – a two-onion curry; *do* meaning two and *pyaz* meaning onion. Strict interpretation of this means adding onion to the preparation in two different forms: ground and fried.

Dosais – pancakes made of ground rice and lentils or farina. Especially popular in the South for breakfast.

Dum – a cooking process in which live charcoal is placed on the lid of the cooking vessel so that the heat comes from above as well as below and the food is cooked by steam.

Elachi – cardamom.

Enghatie – most universal cooking stove in India.

Falooda – a sweetened milk drink.

Foogath – a cooked vegetable dish, usually containing coconut.

Gajar – carrot.

Garam masala – a mixture of spices.

Gaujas – deep fried twists which are dipped in syrup and sprinkled with cardamom.

Ghee – clarified butter.

Ghol – buttermilk.

Gobi – cauliflower.

Gosht – meat.

Gulab jamon – a delicious sweet consisting of small balls made of dried milk which are deep fried and then soaked in a rose- or cardamom-flavored syrup.

Groundnut – peanut

Gur – unrefined cane sugar.

Haldi – turmeric.

Halva – a sweet pudding which can be made of farina, eggs, bananas, beets, carrots, any kind of nut, or just plain flour, and combined with butter, sugar and milk.

Hing – asafetida.

Hoppers – a favorite breakfast item in Madras. A pancake served with coconut milk; also known as appums.

Idlis – South Indian steamed rice cakes; frequently served for breakfast.

Imlee – tamarind.

Jaggery – unrefined cane sugar.

Jaiphul – nutmeg.

Jallahs – earthenware jars used for storing water.

Jallebis – a yellow, crispy circular sweet which has been deep fried and then soaked in syrup and which remains crispy.

Javitri – mace.

Jeera – cumin.

Jhinga – prawns or shrimp.

Jowari – barley.

Kagina – an Indian omelet.

Kajo – cashew nut.

Kaleja – liver.

Kali mirch – black pepper.

Kalonji – tiny black seeds rather like onion seeds.

Kangan – deep-fried little cakes like doughnuts.

Karanjia – deep-fried little cakes filled with raisins and coconut.

Karahi – deep round pan used for deep-fat frying.

Karela – bitter gourd.

Katories – food cups which are placed on the thalis or food trays.

Kayla – banana.

Keema – ground meat.

Kesar – saffron.

Kheer – a pudding made of rice.

Kheera – cucumber.

Khoa – fresh whole milk which has been allowed to evaporate by boiling to a semi-solid consistency. This is used in many Indian sweets.

Khoobanee – dried apricot.

Kismis – raisins.

Kitchri – dish made of rice and dhal (lentils). It originated as an invalid dish and now there are ever so many variations.

Koela – charcoal.

Kofta – a ball. Usually a meatball or vegetable ball.

Koitha – knives for cutting meat.

Korma – a rich curry, usually containing yogurt.

Kuddoo – pumpkin.

Kulfi – a frozen milk sweet.

Kus-kus – poppy seeds.

Kutta – acid.

Laddoo – sweet balls made of any number of lentil flours, farina, nuts or sesame.

Lal mirch – red chili.

Lasan – garlic.

Lassi – a refreshing drink made of buttermilk.

Laung – cloves.

Luchi – deep-fried bread; Bengali equivalent of the poori.

Machi – fish.

Maida – white flour.

Maize – corn.

Malai – cream.

Malayalee – native of Kerala state.

Malpuras – dessert pancakes; sometimes almonds, sesame seeds or cardamom are added. Occasionally soaked in thick syrup or milk before being served.

Masala – spices.

Matar – peas.

Mawa – same as khoa; dried milk.

Methi – fenugreek.

Moilee – a meat, fish, vegetable or egg dish with coconut milk as the base. Very popular in South India.

Mooli – white radish.

Moorga – cock.

Moorgee – fowl.

Murgh masalum – spiced chicken.

Nan – a North Indian leavened baked bread; especially popular with tandoori chicken.

Nariyal – coconut.

Narrangee – orange.

Nimbu – lime.

Pachadi – a mixture of yogurt and vegetables such as cucumber, onion, tomato, eggplant or banana which can be salty or sweet. Very popular in South India as appetizers.

Pakoras – vegetable fritters.

Palak – spinach.

Pani – water.

Panir – a cheese preparation made by curdling milk and

draining out the excess moisture. This product is the base of many Indian sweets.

Paratha – rich, flaky, shallow-fried bread.

Payasam – a sweet pudding-like preparation made with milk and any cereal, lentil or nut.

Phirni – a pudding made of rice or rice flour.

Phulka – a bread; also known as a chappati.

Poodina – mint.

Poori – small round bread made of whole wheat or a mixture of white and whole wheat flour and deep-fat fried.

Poppadums – very crisp wafer-like bread eaten throughout India. Are usually made from lentil and rice flour.

Pulao – a rice preparation which may contain meat, fish or vegetables. The rice is usually fried before it is steamed.

Pyaz – onion.

Rai – mustard.

Raita – a mixture of yogurt and vegetables such as cucumber, potato or cabbage served as an appetizer or salad.

Rasam – a tart, spicy soup of South India. Made with lentils and frequently known as "pepper water."

Rasgullas – sweet, rose-flavored balls made of pannir (Indian cream cheese) and cooked in a sugar syrup.

Rava – farina.

Rogan Josh – a popular North Indian lamb curry.

Roti – bread.

Saar – a curry with plenty of liquid.

Sabz mirch – green chili.

Sag – vegetable preparation made of leafy vegetables such as turnip greens, mustard greens or spinach.

Sambhar – a hot South Indian soup made of lentils and vegetables; usually eaten with dosais, idlis or rice.

Samosa – a small pastry stuffed with ground meat or cooked vegetables and eaten as a snack or appetizer.

Sas – a Parsi dish.

Saunf – aniseed.

Sayoo – apples.

Sewian – a very fine vermicelli used in desserts.

Shahi tukra – a sweet preparation made with fried toast as the base.

Shakarpara – deep-fried bits of dough eaten as snacks.

Shalgam – turnip.

Shami kabab— very popular cutlets made of ground meat and ground lentils.

Shrikand – a sweetened yogurt.

Sirka – vinegar.

Sont – dry ginger.

Soojee – semolina or farina.

Soor – pig.

Sukke – relatively dry curry.

Tandoor – a cylindrical clay oven 4 or 5 feet high in which poultry, meat and fish are barbecued and nan (a bread) is baked.

Tandoori – refers to the meat or fish that is barbecued.

Tawa – heavy griddle used for baking bread and dosais.

Tejpata – bay leaves or cassia leaves.

Til oil – sesame seed oil.

Thali – circular tray on which food is served and eaten.

Udrak – green ginger.

Unday – eggs.

Uppuma – a South Indian breakfast dish made of farina.

Vadas – small cakes or doughnut-shaped snacks made of ground lentils or farina and deep-fat fried. Served with chutney. Very popular in South India.

Yakni – stock.

Zarda – a sweet rice preparation.

BOOKS CONSULTED

INDEX

BOOKS CONSULTED

The Bible: Old and New Testaments

Clair, Colin. *Of Herbs and Spices.* New York: Abelard, 1961.

Encyclopaedia Britannica

Hayes, Elizabeth. *Herbs, Flavours and Spices.* London: Faber and Faber, 1961.

Hemphill, Rosemary. *Spice and Savour.* London: Angus, 1965.

LaWall, C. H. *Four Thousand Years of Pharmacy.* Philadelphia: Lippincott, 1927.

Leyel, C. F. *The Magic of Herbs.* London: J. Cape, 1926.

Redgrove, H. S. *Spices and Condiments.* New York: Pitman, 1933.

Ridley, Henry N. *Spices.* London: Macmillan, 1912.

Walsh, J. J. *Medieval Medicine.* London: A. C. Black, 1920.

INDEX

Adrak (ginger), 19
Alcoholic beverages, 7–8, 35
Allspice, 14, 22
Aloo matar (potato and pea curry), 133
Aloo palak (potatoes and spinach), 134
Amti (lentils), 162
Anda halva, 217
Anise, 13
Aniseed, 13
Aphrodisiacs, 15, 18
Appams (hoppers), 181
Asafetida, 13
Avial (vegetable curry), 9, 128

Banana, halva, 217
  leaves, 33
  pachadi, 190
  pooris, 179
Beans, green, see Green beans
Bean sprouts (titori), 130
Beckti (fish), 103
Beef
  in Kofta curry, 59
  restrictions against, 8, 57
Beer, 35
Bengali curried vegetables, 128
Betel nut, 35
Beverages, to serve, 35
Bhakri (fried bread), 180
Bhath (rice dish), tomato, 42
  Vangi, 44

Bhaturas (fried bread), 180
Bhel poori (snack), 213
Bhendi (okra)
  seasoned, 146
  stuffed, 146
Bhujjia, cauliflower, 137
  tomato and onion, 151
Bhurta, eggplant, 123
  potato, 131
  tomato, 151
Biryani (rice dish), 39
  chicken, 51
  fish, 53
  lamb, 54
  moglai, 52
Black pepper, 12
Bombloe (fish), 102
Bread, 174–182
  appams (hoppers), 181
  banana pooris, 179
  bhakri, 180
  bhaturas, 180
  chappatis, 174
  forms of, 8
  in Indian meals, 34
  luchi, 179
  nan, 177
  paratha, 175
  poori, 178
  poppadums, 182
  spicy potato pooris, 178
  stuffed paratha, 176
Breakfast, South India, 9

Burfi (sweets), 214, 219
Butter, clarified (ghee), 28
Buttermilk curry, 163

Cabbage, foogath, 140
    raita, 192
    salad, Indian, 192
    spicy, 140
Cakes (vadas), 210–211
Candy
    coconut, 229
    see also Desserts and sweets
Capsicums (cayenne pepper and
    chilies), 13
Cardamoms, 12, 15–16
Carrot, halva, 218
    salad, 195
Cashew nut(s)
    halva, 216
    Indian style, 205
    South Indian chicken curry
    with, 83
Cauliflower
    bhujjia, 137
    curry, 136
    lamb with, 66
    and pea raita, 192
    with peas and tomatoes, 137
    pickle, 186
    and potatoes, North Indian
    style, 139
    with raisins, 138
    with yogurt, 138
Cayenne pepper, 12–14, 22
Chappati(s) (bread), 8, 32, 34
    baking of, 174
Chicken, 8, 58, 83–97
    baked, with spiced yogurt, 92
    baked spiced, Indian style, 85
    biryani, 51

Chicken (cont'd)
    with coconut milk and eggs,
    91–92
    with coconut slivers, 93
    coconut soup, 158
    fried, Indian, I, 83
    fried, Indian, II, 84
    with green peas, 95
    with new potatoes, 96
    spicy (murgh masalam), 87
    with sweet potatoes, 89
    tandoori (barbecued), 93
    curry
        with greens, 94
        Kerala coastal, 90
        mild, with potatoes, 87
        pepper, 86
        South Indian, with cashew
        nuts, 83
        spicy, 95
        tomato, 90
    vindaloo, 97
Chick-peas, spicy, 160
Chili con carne, 14
Chilies, 13
    green, 27
Chili peppers, green, 27
Chili powder, 14
Chinese parsley (coriander), 27
Choori (knife), 4
Chudva (snack), 205
Chutney, 9, 197–201
    authentic, 34
    coconut, for idlis, 198
    coconut and coriander leaf, 200
    coriander, 199
    date, 199
    Major Grey's, 34
    mint, 199
    orange and date, 197

Chutney (*cont'd*)
  peanut, 200
  pineapple, 198
  raisin, 200
Cilantro (coriander leaves), 27
Cinnamon, 12, 16
Cinnamon tree, 16
Clarified butter (ghee), 28
Cleanliness, food and, 7–8
Cloves, 12, 14, 16–17
Clove trees, 16
Coconut, 26
  candy, 229
  chutney, 198
    and coriander leaf, 200
    for idlis, 201
  eggs with, 167
  fried lamb and, 67
  milk, 9, 26–27
    and eggs, chicken with, 91
    eggplant in, 125
    fish with, 112
    lamb and green peas in, 74
  moong dhal (lentils), 159
  oil, 28
  rice, 45
  soup, chicken, 158
  shrimp curry with, 119
  spicy potatoes and, 134
  squares, 225
Cod, 103
Coffee, 35
  Indian, 9
Cooking stoves, 4–5, 8, 58, 174
Coriander, 12, 18, 27
  chutney, 199
  leaves, 27–28
  rasam (soup), 154
Corn vadas (cakes), 211
Cow, veneration of, 8, 57

Crab curry, 119
Cuchumber
  cucumber, 197
  onion, 197
  papaya, 196
  tomato, 196
Cucumber, curry, 148
  lamb-stuffed, 69
  pickle, Parsi style, 184
  salad, Parsi, 194
  soup, South Indian, 12, 18–19, 157
Cumin, 12, 18–19
  kababs, 81
Cumin rasam (soup), 157
Curry, 59–61
  Bengali curried vegetables, 128
  beverages with, 35
  buttermilk, 163
  cauliflower, 136
  chicken, 87, 90, 94–95
  crab, 119
  cucumber, 148
  defined, 2–3, 11
  duck, 97
  egg, 164, 166, 172
  egg and split pea, 169
  egg and vegetable, 170
  eggplant, 125
  fish, 103, 105–106, 109–110
  forms of, 58
  ginger in, 20, 148
  keema (meat), 68
  Kerala ginger, 148
  lamb, 62–63, 72–73
  lime, 127
  liver, 78
  pea and potatoes, 133
  potato ball, 135
  potato korma, 130

Curry (*cont'd*)
powder, 11–12
rice and, 8
shrimp, 116–119
spicy mixed vegetable, 141–142
topping for, 34
vegetable, 9, 128, 141–142, 170
vegetable and egg, 170

Dahi, potatoes, 131
see also Yogurt
Dahimachi (fish with yogurt), 106
Darchini (cinnamon), 16
Date chutney, 199
Daughters, training for, 5
Degchis (saucepans), 3
Desserts and sweets, 214–230
anda halva, 217
banana halva, 217
burfi, 219
carrot halva, 218
cashew nut halva, 216
coconut candy, 229
coconut squares, 225
doodh pak, 225
egg halva, 217
falooda, 227
gaujas, 229
gulab jaman, 215
jallebis, 222
kulfi, 219
malpuras (pancakes), 226
nut and sesame ladoo, 223
phirni, 221
rasgullas, 220
regional variations in, 8
semolina ladoo, 224
sewian, 224
shahi tukra, 221

Desserts (*cont'd*)
shakarpara, 223
shrikand, 228
vermicelli payasam, 228
zarda, 227
Dhal (lentils), 8–9, 34, 152
coconut moong, 159
with split yellow peas, 162
sukke, 155
urid, 30, 210
Dhan sak, 10
Dhannia (coriander), 18
Doodh pak, 225
Do pyaz, lamb, 71
Dosais (pancakes), 208–209
masala, 209
rava, 208
rice, 209
Duck, 97–101
baked, and vegetables, 100
buffado, 101
curry, spicy, 97
korma, 98
Madras, vindaloo, 98
pepper fried, 99
Dum (charcoal), 5

Egg(s), 164–172
Akuri, 165
baked, with okra, 168
chicken with coconut milk and, 91
with coconut, 167
pickled, 185
and potato curry, 166
rice, 41
spicy, 171
and split pea curry, 168
taboos against, 7–8

Egg(s) (*cont'd*)
  tomato and, 169
  vegetable curry and, 170
Eggplant
  bhurta, 123
  in coconut milk, 125
  curry, 125
  Kerala theeyal, 126
  pachadi, 191
  rice and, 44
  spicy, 122
  stuffed, Indian style, 124
  with yogurt, 123
Elachi (cardamon), 15
Ericheri (pumpkin and yogurt), 9, 141
Enghatie (cooking stove), 4–5
Equivalents and substitutions, 31

Falooda, 227
Fats and oils, 28–29
Fenugreek, 12, 19
Fish and other seafood, 102–120
  baked, in leaves (Patrani machhi), 107
  baked, Malayalee style, 112
  biryani, 53
  with coconut milk, 112
  curry, 109–110
    Bengal style, 103
    Coastal, 106
    spicy and sour, 105
    tomato, 110
  fried, Kerala style, 108
  fried spiced, 109, 111
  kalia, 104
  pappas, Malayalee, 110
  sas, Parsi, 113
  taboos against, 8

Fish (*cont'd*)
  with tomatoes, 108
  with tomato yogurt sauce, 104
  with yogurt (dahimachi), 106
  see also Flounder, etc.
Flounder, 103
Flours, 6, 173–174
  lentil, 29
  rice, 29
Food
  Indian customs and beliefs about, 7–8
  regional variations in, 8–10
  rules relating to, 7–8, 32–33
  taboos concerning, 33, 57–58
Foogath, cabbage, 140
  green bean, 149

Garlic, 14
Gaujas (dessert), 229
Ghee (clarified butter), 28
Ginger, 12, 19
  curry, Kerala, 148
  pachadi, 189
Goat meat, 8
Green beans, fried, Indian style, 149
  foogath, 149
Green peppers, 27
  Indian stuffed, 129
Grilled meats, 8
Grinding stone, 4
Guinea pepper, 22
Gujarat region, food variations in, 9
Gulab jaman (dessert), 215

Haldi (turmeric), 24
Halibut, 103

Halva, 9, 21
  anda, 217
  banana, 217
  carrot, 218
  cashew nut, 216
  egg, 217
Hands and mouth, washing of, 35
Hindu belief
  symbolism of cow in, 57
  food customs and, 7–8
  serving and eating customs, 33
Hing (asafetida), 13
Household duties, training in, 5–6

Idlis (rice cakes), 9, 211
  coconut chutney for, 201
Indad, lamb, 71
India
  beliefs about food in, 7–8
  climate of, 2, 232
  contrasts in, 231
  household management in, 5–6
  kitchens and equipment in, 3–5
  languages, 232
  population of, 231
  rainfall, 232
  religions in, 232
  vegetarians in, 7
Indian cookery, origins of, 1–2
Indian food
  popular beliefs about, 2–3
  serving and eating of, 32–33
Indian meals
  composition of, 34–35
  suggested menus for, 35–36
  "typical," 8

Jaiphul (nutmeg), 21
Jallahs (water jars), 4
Jallebis (dessert), 222

Jamaica pepper, 22
Jammu lamb, 64
Javriti (mace), 21
Jeera (cumin), 19
Jhal faraezi (lamb and potatoes), 73

Kababs, 8
  cumin, 81
  kathi, 82
  liver, 82
  seekh, 81
  shami, 80
  spicy, 79
Kalan (bananas in yogurt), 150
Kalia, fish, 104
Kali mirch (black pepper), 23
Karahi (pan for frying), 4
Karcom (saffron), 23
Katoris (cups), 33
Keema curry, 58, 68
Kerala coastal chicken curry, 90
  ginger curry, 148
  theeyal (eggplant dish), 126
Kerosene stoves, 5
Kesar (saffron), 24
Khagina (egg dish), 166
Khoa (whole milk), 215
Kidneys, lamb and, 64
Kitchens and equipment, 3–5
Kitchri (rice dish), 55
Knife and fork, nonuse of, 33
Kofta, 58
  curry, 59
    Nargisi, 61
Koitha (knife), 4
Korma, curry, lamb, 62
  meat, 58
Kulfi (dessert), 219

Ladoo (dessert), 214
  nut and sesame, 223
  semolina, 224
Lamb, 8, 59–77
  bafat, 77
  baked marinated, 66
  biryani, 54
  with cauliflower, 66
  curry, 8, 62–63
    korma, 62
    mild, 72
    South Indian, 73
  cutlets, Indian style, 76
  do pyaz, 71
  fried, with coconut, 67
  and green peas with coconut milk, 74
  indad, 71
  leg of, Muslim style, 70
  masala, with green beans, 75
  and potatoes (jhal faraeze), 73
  pulao with, 49
Laung (cloves), 17
Lemon pickle, 186
Lentil flour, 29
Lentils, 9
Lentils and soups, 152–163
Licorice, 13
Lime pickle, 185
Lime rice, 41
Liquor, taboo on, 7–8, 35
Liver curry, 78, 127
  kababs, 82
  spicy fried, 77
Luchi (bread), 179

Mace, 12, 20
  see also Nutmeg and mace
Madras duck vindaloo, 99

Madras omelet curry, 167
Maharashtra, food variations in, 9–10
Malpuras (sweet pancakes), 226
Mango
  pickle I, 187
  pickle II, 188
  pickle with peanuts, 188
  salad, 195
Margarine, 28
Marinated lamb, 66
Masala (spices), 12
  dosais, 203
  idli, 212
  lamb shanks, 75
Meals, serving and eating of, 32–33
  see also Indian meals
Meat, 57–101
  grilled, 8
  taboos against, 8, 57–58
  see also Beef; Chicken; Lamb
Meatball curry, 59, 61
Meatballs, 59
Meat korma, 58
Melegueta pepper, 22
Menus, suggested, 55–56
Methi (fenugreek), 19
Mint chutney, 199
Moglai biryani, 52
Moilee, egg, 171
  South Indian vegetable, 144
Mooli (radish stuffing), 176
Mortar and pestle, 4, 12
Mulligatawny soup, 152, 158
Murgh masalum (spicy chicken), 87–88
Muslims, food taboos of, 7–8
Mustard, 20–21

Mustard seed oil, 20–21, 28

Nan (bread), 8, 58, 174
  baking of, 177
Nargisi meatball curry, 61
North Indian lamb and kidneys, 64
North Indian lamb curry (rogan josh), 63–64
Nut cutlets, 212
Nut and sesame ladoo, 223
Nutmeg and mace, 21
Nutmeg tree, 21

Oils, 28–29
  coconut, 28
  mustard seed, 20–21, 28
  olive, nonuse of, 29
  peanut, 29
  sesame seed, 28
  vegetable, 29
Oil stoves, 5
Okra
  baked eggs and, 168
  patia, shrimp and, 117
  sas, 145
  seasoned, 146
  stuffed, 146
Olan (squash), 9, 147
Omelet, 165
  curry, 167
Onion(s)
  cuchumber, 197
  pachadi, 190
  potatoes and, 132
  raita, 193
  spicy, 147
  and yogurt salad, 194

Orange and date chutney, 198
Oregano, 14

Paan, 35
Pachadi (seasoned yogurt), 9, 184
  banana, 190
  eggplant, 191
  ginger, 189
  onion, salt version, 190
    sweet version, 190
  tomato, 191
Pakoras (vegetable fritters), 206
Palak sag (spiced spinach puree), 145
Pancakes
  malpuras (Indian sweet), 226
  rava dosais, 208
  rice dosais, 209
Papaya cuchumber, 196
Pappas, Malayalee fish, 110
Paprika, 14, 30
Parathas (bread), 8, 34, 174
  baking of, 175
  stuffed, 176
Parsi cucumber salad, 194
Parsi fish sas, 113
Parsi omelet, 165
Patia, shrimp and okra, 117
Patrani machhi (fish baked in leaves), 107
Payasam (pudding), 9
  vermicelli, 228
Pea, split, *see* Split pea
Peanut chutney, 200
Peanut oil, 29
Peanuts, mango pickle with, 188
Peas, with cauliflower and tomatoes, 137
Pepper, 22–23

Pepper (cont'd)
  black, 22
  cayenne, see Cayenne pepper
  Guinea, 22
  Melegueta, 22
  red, 22
  Saigon, 23
  white, 22
Pepper water, 156
"Pepper water soup," 152, 158
Peppers
  green, see Green peppers
  red, 13
Phirni (milk dessert), 9, 221
Phulka (bread), 174
Pickle
  cauliflower, 186
  cucumber, Parsi style, 184
  lime, 185
  mango I, 187
  mango II, 188
  mango with peanuts, 188
  sweet lemon, 186
Pickled eggs, 185
Pilaff (rice), 38–39
  see also Rice
Pimento, 22
Pimienta, 14
Pimientos, 13
Pimms cup, 35
Pineapple chutney, 198
Plates, nonuse of, 33
Pomfret (fish), 103
Poori(s), 34, 174
  baking of, 178
  banana, 179
  Bhel, 213
  potato, 178
Poppadums (poppas), 29, 34, 182

Poppy seeds, 30
Pork, taboo against, 7–8
Pork vindaloo, 79
Potato(es)
  balls, curried, 135
  bhurta, 131
  cauliflower and, North Indian
    style, 139
  cauliflower and rice, 46
  curry, eggs and, 166
  dahi, 131
  korma, 130
  with onions and tomatoes, 132
  and pea curry (aloo matar), 133
  pooris, spicy, with coconut, 178
  raita, 192
  and spinach (aloo palak), 134
  with tomatoes, 135
  yogurt and, 132
Poultry, 57–101
  see also Chicken; Duck
Pulao (rice), 8, 38–39
  green peas and, 49
  with lamb, 49
  plain, 46
  shrimp, 48
  tomato, 47
  vegetable, 50
Pulse, 19
Pumpkin, 9
  yogurt and (erisheri), 141

Raan (Muslim style leg of lamb),
  70
Rai (mustard), 21
Raisin chutney, 200
Raisins, cauliflower with, 138
Raita (seasoned yogurt), 9
  cabbage and, 192

Raita (*cont'd*)
  cauliflower and pea, 192
  onion, 193
  potato, 192
  spinach, 193
  see also Yogurt
Rasam (lentil soup), 9
Rasgullas (dessert), 220
Rava dosais (pancakes), 208
Red peppers, 13
Relishes, 183–201
Rice, 8, 37–56
  boiled, 40
  bread made from, 173
  coconut, 45
  cultivation of, 37–38
  egg, 41
  and eggplant, 44
  lime, 41
  potatoes, cauliflower and, 46
  preparation of, 38–40
  raw, 38
  regional variations in, 9
  serving of, 32–33
  sesame, 44
  steamed, 39
  tomato (tomato bhath), 42
  at weddings, 38
  yogurt and, 42
  see also Pulao
Rice cakes (idlis), 211
Rice flour, 12, 29
Rogan josh (lamb curry), 8, 58, 63
Roller, 4

Saffron, 23–24
Sag, Palak, 145

Saigon pepper, 23
Sak, okra, 145
  Parsi fish, 113
Salads, 194–197
  cabbage, 195
  onion and yogurt, 194
  Parsi cucumber, 194
Sambhar (lentils), 3, 9, 153, 203
Samosas (pastry), 203
Sanghara (fish), 103
Saunf (aniseed), 13
Seekh kababs, 81
Seer (fish), 103
Semolina ladoo, 224
Serving and eating customs, 32–33
Sesame rice, 44
Sesame seed oil, 28
Sewian (vermicelli), 224
Shahi tukra (dessert), 221
Shakarpara (dessert), 223
Shami kababs, 80
Shastras, 7
Shopping list, 30
Shrikand (dessert), 10, 228
Shrimp, 102, 114–119
  curry, 118
    with coconut milk, 117
    Goanese style, 116
    hot, with coconut, 119
    mild, 118
  and okra patia, 117
  patia, 115
  pulao, 48
  spiced with potatoes, 114
  spicy, 114
  vindaloo, 115
Snacks, 202–213
Sole (fish), 103
Sont (ginger), 19

Sooji vadas (cakes), 210
Soups and lentils, 152–163
  amti, 162
  buttermilk curry, 163
  chicken coconut, 158
  coconut moong dhal, 159
  coriander rasam, 154
  cumin rasam, 157
  dhal, 162
  Indian split pea, 161
  mulligatawny, 152, 158
  pepper water, 156
  sambhar, 153
  South Indian cucumber, 157
  spicy chick-pea, 160
  sukke dhal, 155
  tomato and lime rasam, 155
  urid dhal, 30
Soy sauce, 13
Spiced baked chicken, 85
  see also Chicken
Spice Islands, 21
Spices
  grinding of, 12
  masala, 12
  most frequently used, 11–24
  reason for using, 2
Spicy chicken (murgh masalum), 87
  stuffed, 88
Spinach
  lamb with, 76
  puree, spiced (palak sag), 145
  raita, 193
  with yogurt, 144
Split pea curry, egg and, 169
Split peas, spiced, 206
Split pea soup, 161
Squash, 147

Stewed lamb with tomatoes and potatoes, 65
Storage canister, 3–4
Stoves, types of, 4–5, 58, 174
Substitutions and equivalents, 31
Sukke dhal (lentils), 155
Sweet potatoes, chicken with, 89
Sweets, see Desserts and sweets

Taboos, concerning food, 7–8, 33, 57–58.
Tandoor (oven), 58, 174
Tandoori chicken, 93, 174
Tandoori cooking, 8, 58
Tawa (heavy griddle), 4
Tea, 35
Thali (tray), 33
Titori (bean sprouts), 130
Tomato(es)
  bhath, 42
  bhurta, 151
  with cauliflower and peas, 137
  chicken curry, 90
  cuchumber, 196
  eggs, spicy, 169
  fish curry, 110
  and lime rasam, 155
  and onions (bujjia), 151
  pachadi, 191
  potatoes and, 132, 134
  pulao, 47
  rice, 42
Turmeric, 12, 24

Urid dhal, (lentil), 30, 210, 212
Uppuma (snack), 207
  cinnamon, 208
  tomato, 208

Vadas, corn, 211
  sooji, 210
Vangi bhath (rice and eggplant),
  44
Vegetable(s), 121–151
  Bengali curried, 128
  curry, 8, 141
  egg and, 170
  fritters (pakoras), 206
  mixed, 141–143
  mixed, in tomato sauce, 143
  moilee, South Indian, 144
  oil, 29
  pulao, 50
  taboos, 7
  and yogurt, 184
  see also Spinach, etc.
Vegetarian menu, 36
Vermicelli payasam (dessert), 228
Vindaloo, chicken, 97
  Madras duck, 99
  shrimp, 115

Water, pepper, 156
Water, serving of, 33
Wheat, 7, 173
Wine, incorrectness of, 35
Women, role of, in household,
  5–7

Yellow rice, 43
Yogurt, 9
  cauliflower with, 138
  eggplant with, 123
  potatoes in, 132
  pumpkin and, 141
  spiced, chicken baked with,
    92
  spinach with, 144
  see also Pachadi; Raita
Yogurt rice, 42

Zarda (dessert), 227